CARIAD

LIVING AS LOVE

Sara Jane Hunter

© Copyright 2021

By Sara Jane Hunter

All rights reserved. No part of this book may be reproduced by any means, except for brief excerpts for the purpose of reviews, without the express permission of the publisher.

ISBN: 978-1-914408-60-1

Cover picture by Hannah Salisbury

This book is dedicated to my four children: Harriet, James, Thomas and Will. May you grow to fully express the Divine essence that fills us all. I am so grateful for all the learning and encouragement from the many beautiful beings who have informed the stories within this book. To my husband Mark, for his infinite patience and teaching me to accept love!

FOREWARD by Diederik Wolsak RCP, MPCP

CARIAD: Living as Love

Sara Hunter's new book, Cariad, is a message of hope, of love and of courageous commitment to healing. What is it that needs to be healed? As Sara illustrates, with insight and compassion, it is the false, small 's' self, the ego self. She beautifully illustrates how that little self came into being and she shows - with authority derived from a lifetime of experience - that you and I do not need to live with that self any longer. That little self has brought us anxiety, depression, crippling fears and a deep sense of loneliness. Not only that but that self has also led so many of us to conflicts, financial distress and dysfunctional relationships.

What a wonderfully written book, with a profound blending of poetry and mysticism balanced by the obvious gifts found in many years of working with families in crisis. Sara's primary commitment is to heal the self. She knows like few others that no true healing can take place if the 'healing' is seen and pursued in the 'other'. All healing is self-healing and Sara brings that message with a simple directness which is both moving and inspiring.

I am grateful to Sara for her work 'in the field', for her huge heart, her intelligence and for being such a clear minded student and teacher to us all.

Prologue

If you are searching for the ideal partner, looking for the right job, trying to decide where to live and how to follow your passion or your dreams, then this is the book for you! If you have decisions to make or you feel stuck, asking the 'what next?' question then read on. If none of the above applies then still look because you may find a gift within these pages.

After many years of exploring and pondering those questions and the searching, with the constant requests of 'show me', how can I find the answers? Where are the answers? I was asking these questions to find answers beyond those that are a given. Beyond the path of leaving school, get a job, marry, have children, retire and die.

Two years of non-stop downloads of information and with every book full of poems and prose, there was still this same question. The writing was exquisite and filled with inspiration but then finally the answer was delivered in one word: CARIAD, a journey or a path that you too can take. Cariad comes as a direct transmission of love and hope that we can all feel and utilise as we connect up to the full power that lies within the cells of our bodies. Now there lies a path, we can optimise to find our true power and purpose in life which is love. Our future requires that we all share our gifts with one another with open hearts. Following this journey, my greatest wish is that you will find your own heart fully opened and all of our latent compassion will in turn be released into our world. Here lies the hope for all our children and future generations that will walk this earth. Now is the time of the greatest awakening that has ever been witnessed, the one prophesied by every world religion and by the Native Americans, the Aborigines and all the wise elders of our nations.

This is a journey that you can take for yourself or with others but come with an open mind, be inquisitive and curious. Maybe even remove all the critical thinking and give yourself permission to delve between these pages in tune with an expansive consciousness, an open-hearted awareness of the modern-day mystic.

WORDS FOR REFLECTION

Universal living intelligence is dynamic, a moving and loving force, with nothing to do and nowhere to go; for this is the divine universal consciousness that we all live and breathe. All we have to do is to gather our senses about us, as we move through life and it gently flows in and out and returns to the earth and the cosmos. Feel the peace rising on the incoming tide of gratitude and be 'at one' with all that is.

For to be against, to protect or defend are the old platitudes of long ago, they cut us off from fully showing up and being in the here and now, we share the same divine living intelligence that connects every living being. For Cariad connects, as you are the Beloved, the Sweetheart, that Loved One that you have longed for, it is you, as you embrace your 'I AM Presence' (truly feeling within the Oneness and universal Presence of Love) as you soak up the loving elixir, that fills every sentient being. To be fully awake as a human is to remember the Truth, that we are all connected in Love, by Love and for Love. How wonderous is that? Take it in, just for a moment, rest in that space and feel the everlasting Peace that is ours. It is the beauty that guides the brush of the painter, fills the page of the writer and lifts the feet of the dancer. Move on and experience the magnificence of our lives, divine and roaring as the crashing waves upon the dawning of this new era.

Our swimming consciousness, it is like our awareness is a sea of energy that is always moving. How to ride the waves that run in and out with the tides; with the body as a vessel, our energy container. The biggest challenge we all face is to be the master of the energies that we encounter every day. How we do this is going to be different for each of us, as we are all unique, but it is essential for our Evolution that we can master this.

How beautiful it is to be human, to observe the velocity, the rise and fall; I notice how my mind can run off on currents of energy all over the place. I catch these runaway streams of unconscious thought and bring them back to the main river of energy that is my own direct connection to Source energy. Directing the flow to align or tap into the currents of the epic and eternal supply of Universal Consciousness. This meets and mingles with my own flow and gives those power surges that pulsate through my human body.

> **It is in the aliveness, the full-on vitality, of a life lived flat out I find you**
> **As I dance and write, there you are....**

In my falling into bliss and ecstasy there you are
It's the open-ended divine consciousness that bathes all of life,
There you are in the sweet marigolds and chestnut tree
Reaching branches that caress the sky
Green wetlands with wild geese a flight
Open wings enchanting the landscape
magical luminosity of swan upon lake
gliding effortlessly as the bee's hum
buzzing about their business of nectar gathering,
drawing luscious life from every open flower,
The bees are sacred.
How they guide us to our own path of Sovereignty,
of being at one with nature and our world,
together in unison, they work for the good of all.
Take a spoon of honey and taste upon your tongue

the visceral experience of life lived fully in
Service to the Divine, here lies the secret for
mankind.
In the hustle and bustle of chaotic life, let us
slow down,
Watch the bees.
Listen to the birdsong and savour the life
That so beautifully surrounds us
Take just a moment to breathe it all in
and exhale the wonder of nature.
Be amazed and sit on the earth as you feel

the wonderous gifts that are there,
beneath our feet, above us, all around us
be at peace now,
In our most divine and sacred land.

The poem serves to remind us all that we are in connection all of the time, to the birds and the bees and in our embryonic stage, in the womb. In the waters of the womb, we begin our life, we grow from the single organ of the heart into an entire being, then we are born. We take our first breath of creative life force for ourselves and now we have our own connection.

INTRODUCTION: The Origins of Cariad

The river of life is flowing…

What a gift it is to realise that the flow of energy is unlimited, it is just a case of tuning into it and re-connecting to this Divine intelligence. It's like a sweet spot, which we can all locate, I find it when I am dancing, it is from this place that I can pick up my pen and begin writing:

A few years ago, walking upon the shoreline in Mulranny, Ireland, I heard the words of a song being sung to me:

**The river of life is flowing through the waters of the womb…
The mystery of life lies in the waters of the womb.**

The song was sung over and over until the song somehow emerged into my being. I had often pondered what was this? I had heard about Soul Songs, with a message from our Higher Self; but really, from a human perspective, this made no sense. This was not going to be something that my mind could explain, but gradually an awareness began to dawn. There is this notion of me, as a human being, and then there is an awareness that I am also the Divine Creator of life; both the Creation and the Creator. Whatever your beliefs may be, have an open mind and feel how this resonates, "the river of life is flowing through the waters of the womb".

Several years after I had heard these words, I had been attending a workshop in Stratford-Upon-Avon. You know, Shakespeare was born here and one of his most well-known quotes is; **'All the world's a stage and every man and woman, merely players'.** For sure we are all learning the game of life and we all have a part to play. What part might we be playing?

Well, as I was driving my car along the M4, towards home in Wales, a voice began speaking clearly to me, and telling me to pull over the car, as I needed to write something down. As I picked up my pen, I was told that I was going to write a book that would guide others how to connect directly with Source. There was a very lengthy description of all that the book needed to contain and all the titles for chapters. The book was to describe all the ways in which I had felt and found this connection to Source, to enable others to do the same. For a while, I did follow through, writing and connecting with others but there was not a flow, perhaps this was because there was still more to learn, for there is always another layer of the onion to peel and reveal yet further wisdom.

That was until two years ago, when the outline of Cariad became very clear. As you read, you will find you come across a mixture of writing, that of direct connection to Source, Divine Mother/Father Creator Consciousness, where words gather into poems and prose, here there is a flow, and there is an uplift of energy which is experienced as Joy, or complete contentment and Peace or a deep sense of Compassion.

Other times, as I am writing from Sara, as my personality self, it can feel contrite, and I am questioning myself all the time. Not surprising, as I have an imprint of 'self-doubt', probably born of the conflict between those moments of Source flow and then my own personal interpretation, which can at times seem to jar, and leave me feeling somewhat uncertain, worried about what others will be thinking as they read this! Yet this seems to have balanced out on these pages and it will be interesting to see if you notice your own reaction, as two styles of writing flow into one another.

In the same way that our own consciousness flows, present in the now, and then there is flowing or running off into slipstreams of the past or future. Following those conditioned responses or patterns, the well-worn grooves and channels. Here is learning for all of us, for we are, after all, human beings having a divine experience. Noticing when the energy flows and when it becomes stuck.

Noticing when we are held up in habitual thought patterns of the conditioned mind.

Whatever we believe, we have this non-stop energy supply, flowing, like a live current through us. We then look to those around us to guide us, we have all this power and we have to learn how to use it, power on, power off. With all of this powerful energy flowing we are looking for guidance. We are looking and learning from those around us, how to manage the voltage. Or another way of saying this is that we are learning emotional self-management. For what is emotion but energy flowing. We are learning when we can let rip and when we may need to stem the flow.

My Grandson loves to play tennis, he is learning that to fully pelt the ball, he needs to be outside. He does love watching his Mum's shocked look, if the ball does bounce off the kitchen wall, but he knows already, it is best for him to enjoy this game outside. What is he doing? Learning to be the master of his energy. You can see the potential for this to go pear-shaped already if our parents or care-givers themselves have not grasped the essentials of energy management. For we are guiding the flow for our children, all the time they are looking and learning, until the time comes when they are on their own, and running with the energy supply for themselves.

We grow up and we have a pattern of energy flow that we have learned early on in childhood. Now we have all the energy, and how we channel this and flow with it, is going to vary according to the lessons of energy management we have observed. What if the secret to learning to harness this great internal power is that we need to love, to grow and to heal? Essentially to learn that I am the source of power and I am creating my own life.

Energy Flow and Miracles

A question that I started to ask in childhood was about our energy and I was curious, how was it that Jesus healed people? It puzzled me that others were not also doing the same. The answer, so often given, was that 'it was a miracle'. Then I would ask, how was it a miracle? For it occurred to me that we could all do this and yet no one was teaching us how, so I kept on asking.

During contemplation, I was repeatedly asking about miracles, it was like a quest to learn more. Was it possible we could all perform miracles and if so, what has God got to do with this? In the use of the term: God, please know that you can equally replace this with Allah, Buddha, or even Peter Pan, for it is simply a term that describes that consciousness that lies beyond physical form; that breathes all of life.

How can we all become a Clear Channel to fully connect to this Source power was a big Quest. When I look back now, I was provided with many answers, that are gathered into this book. If I was to try to answer that question now, it means: that as we release and let go all of our Ego stories and conditioning, the darkness becomes lighter. We stop fighting ourselves and allow our Consciousness to be Evolved as we witness life through an open heart. We step into our true and authentic power, the light that is divine consciousness. It is not a knowing that our minds can grasp onto for it is a feeling that resonates within the heart. The presence of Love relies on heart connection, a felt experience. rather than a certain mind grasping.

Take every moment and magnify it with Love

For when we are truly living in heart connection, we notice and become aware that we are all connected one to another. Every one of us is born through connection with our mother, as the umbilical cord from her to us, feeds us and breathes us. We are also connected to nature, as we breathe in oxygen from the air. Where does this come from? The trees, the plants and the miracle of photosynthesis. We live in this synthesis of heart connection, all of the time.

Could it be that the only pain and seemingly difficult moments arise in our choice to separate from all that lives and breathes us?

One morning, as I was in the midst of my own spiritual practice, of sacred connection, with rose oils and surrounded by beauty, I was feeling this oneness, the connection within my heart, expanding and opening, throughout my entire body, life was pulsing a huge energy and I became a part of the energy both within and without. I felt an expansive opening through my womb and a direct connection to the primordial womb of the earth. I had read that the womb is like a portal, an entrance to the divinity of all life, but now I had drifted through and became a part of all that is, drifting into utter love and stillness, in a state of complete serenity. Not wanting to move, just sensing that all of life was in fact breathing through me for I had become a Sacred Vessel of Love. That Clear Channel. An exquisite place of 'I Am', where we all are, where I cannot be in it, out of it or indeed part of it for 'I AM divine creator consciousness'. Since this moment, it seems that perception has shifted my awareness far beyond the mere physical form.

The Passage from Birth to Death

Having only ever seen one dead body, all I can say is there was no life force remaining inside that body, it was cold, empty and lifeless. If the lifeforce enters us after birth, and leaves us when we die, are we the lifeforce or the body? That is a question to ponder, but judging by the numbers of those who report, from their own 'near-death experiences', it seems that what lies beyond is the presence of divinity with beautiful light and so much love. Here is that idea of light again, perhaps that is what connects us, the light of consciousness.

A dear colleague of mine, thought she was dying and recalled walking into a long tunnel and as she walked, she was aware that there was a light coming towards her, as the light drew closer, she believed it was God holding the light and he spoke to her with the words: 'I am the light of the world'. This was all the more fascinating because there is a small picture of Christ holding a lamp, which is pinned on the Welsh dresser in our kitchen, and those are the exact words written there too. It was Eckhart Tolle who delivered the idea that the light, so often referred to in the bible, and other religious texts, does in truth refer to consciousness.

This is a lengthy explanation to offer a suggestion that what might in fact connect us all is Consciousness. As we release the Ego thoughts we are lighter, evolving. The question may then become, does this consciousness remain with us and if so, are we all eternal in consciousness? And on a more practical level, how do we evolve our consciousness? How do we become our own beloved and expand and fully open our hearts to enter this new paradigm? On the Cariad journey I hope that you will find some of the answers for yourselves. And find your own path.

Trust your awakening heart, find the peace that is at the core of existence.
Be the light of expanded consciousness,
 and ignite the flame of passion that is within your sacred heart.
Then rest, quite simply, in the spaciousness of love

Chapter One: HOW DOES CARIAD CONNECT?

We all know that we are always in relationship and if connection aids consciousness to evolve, we need to learn more about the ways in which we can all start to connect. For many years, listening to the stories of women who find themselves in Refuge, my question was how do we build positive connections and loving relationships? It is clear that we all know what we don't want, 'let's break the cycle of abuse', we say, and yet the answer, I believe, lies in steering us in the direction of starting a new cycle of how-to live-in peace. This requires that each one of us begins by finding that peace within our own hearts first.

Up until now, the only approaches seem to be geared towards how to stem the flow of abuse. My sense of this is that when we are against something, whatever that might be, we are coming from the wrong place. We have to ask, has what we have done so far worked? The answer is NO, if we look at the numbers of calls that the police receive, regarding domestic abuse, every day, these are increasing. A UK police officer commented recently, that she has never yet worked a shift without a call related to domestic abuse. This is an interesting place to start as domestic abuse affects everyone, from all walks of life, irrespective of race or creed.

We so readily accept the term domestic abuse, what this means is there is a disturbance, within the heart of the home, or a family. We are very complacent in accepting it, so it seems commonplace.

We need to ask the question, if the numbers of cases are increasing, year upon year, in more homes and more families, how else could we look at this? What are we all missing? Asking instead what are we trying to create and achieve? The exact opposite term is 'domestic bliss' or 'domestic calm'. How is peace achieved in couples and families? It could be harmonious relationships, where adults treat one another with respect.

Then the next question could be, how do we create and build relationships that foster loving kindness, rather than abuse? Then we would need to look back at the life of a person, from birth, where do we learn about relationships in the first place? From the cradle, we could say this is where relationships all begin, but in truth, the womb is our first home and there is a lot more to be said about this as a solution for us all. But the first step required is for each one of us to stand in front of a mirror and take a good look at our own reflection and then be honest with what we see. How do we really feel about ourselves? Are we seeing the man or woman of our dreams? Whatever I do not like about myself, those bits that I hide from everyone, those are the very pieces that are getting reflected back at me as I venture out into the world. The first relationship to heal is our very own.

Right now, we are witnessing external chaos, could this very madness be asking us to look within for a new solution? To make peace with ourselves. Facing a whole year with the Pandemic of 2020, that has impacted our entire world, everyone had to stay at home. An opportunity for learning to find out how it is to live with our own company, maybe for the first-time people are really beginning to learn how-to live-in connection. Many have found the answer, the secret that has eluded us for centuries, when we find peace within, we experience the world as peaceful. We start to find an internal rhythm as human beings, and this aligns us to the rhythm of nature and the world outside. We are starting a movement towards birthing a new paradigm. There is a Chinese Proverb:

When there's light in the soul, then there is beauty in a person, when there's beauty in a person then there is harmony in the house, when there's harmony in the house then there's order in the nation and when there's order in the nation then there is peace in the world.

It is clear that we need to change our focus and as Ghandi would say; 'be the change you want to see in the world'. A good place to start is to ask, how do we become the loving, gentle and kind human beings that we would like to meet out there in the world?

How can we follow the natural flow so that we are in alignment with the Source of life force that governs all of existence? When we ask about flow, we are sharing the view of the indigenous peoples, that we are all in connection all of the time. It makes sense then, to be curious about how we lost the connection to the natural harmonious flow of life, and look for ways to reconnect, for us all to exist, once again, in harmony. This is the route we need to take for creating lasting peace in our world. Rather than asking how do we stop or end the violence, let us all begin to look for that answer within, rather than outside of ourselves. It is clear we cannot stem the tide of abuse by doing what we have always done. There is another way, I have witnessed this in my work over the last twenty years.

We have first to create this peace and harmony within ourselves, this changes how we see the world. Then we must share this in our families and in our wider communities. This quest for peace within, to witness peace without, has been the path that we have walked, within our MAMs Community Interest Company, working with mothers and their families.

This book is the telling of a new story... going inside and finding a natural solution for peace. The steps are contained within the word CARIAD, a Welsh word that at a simple level translates as love, (more about this later), and so was born Cariad for a new shift in our evolution, finding within, the universal flow of consciousness that connects us all.

SYMBIOSIS, OUR OWN NATURAL SOLUTION

When we look at life from a Cariad perspective, our hearts are open and our perceptual lenses are all inclusive. We already know this experience within our own DNA for we started life, in symbiotic connection, within the womb of our mothers. This is the place where we must begin, in bringing our heart-open awareness, to look at our planet now. It is interesting that within the human embryo, the heart is the very first organ that forms.

When we look at our world situation, a great question to start asking is how do we extend our heartfelt love into every issue that we face? To find a solution from the heart that brings about a loving resolution. It will feel right if there is an extension of love, bringing with it that loving conscious awareness to find connective and creative solutions, that add love, and bring the compassionate answers to those difficult questions.

For example, in my working day, when a mother is asking for support to raise her child, can we begin to visualise that child always 'resting in love', (see poem A Bed of Human Hearts) then ask, what will it take, right here and now to bring that about? If in pregnancy, a mother is content and at peace, her baby experiences this too. We could make a huge difference by seeing the miracle that is the growing of a baby in the womb and celebrating the joy of motherhood.

We have to be prepared to seek only the most loving gesture that we can make in any given situation, one that joins us together and does not separate us. Always allowing for the continuum of connection which is the idea behind Cariad, returning us into that symbiotic oneness of the womb. After all, are all of our needs not met for us, as we tap into this visceral knowing of what flows through us and breathes us all? We did not have to instruct our bodies, as women, to tell the womb how to develop a baby, any more than we tell our heart how to beat. Universal loving consciousness is just doing this all of the time regardless. When we come together, we can find this symbiosis, for we know it already, and this is where we will find the solution to everything.

It already exists, we just need to reconnect with it. In the same way as my computer is not going to 'power up' until it is plugged into the power source. The supply of our power is generated by love, being in divine flow with universal life. There is so much to be gained if we can rest into loving arms, to connect with love. Notice how people look at a new baby or a kitten, this can re-awaken our natural, loving instinct. Maybe we simply need to remind one another how to love again and see our inherent innocence.

The living essence of connectivity is your essential nature, and yet we have superimposed upon this a set of beliefs about how we need to be and act, according to who we think we have become. When we strip away these layers, beneath this we are still all connected, it is this remembering that is required for our planet and our people. If we take all the natural resources of our world, there is plenty for everyone, no one needs to be hungry or homeless, let us recall the symbiosis, and that natural knowing, of how to share resources for the sustenance, nurture and wellbeing of all. Why are we not sharing? For we should be thriving on our inter-connectivity, as one nation who are of the same clan, the tribe of one heart. For we share the same love and heart connection, we arrived here in the world as a result of sharing that connection, 'making love' with another. Then we gently rest in the womb of our mother, where all of our needs are met. In exactly the same way, Mother Earth meets all of our needs; for we are all of us together, one living organism, each of us a part of the whole. Each of us makes a contribution of love (as our mothers did for us), that unites the forcefield of love that lives and breathes our planet. It is in the living expression of this Love, in connection, that we will all experience an Evolution of Consciousness, that will see us all eventually thriving together.

It is the mothers who bring each soul into the world, we know this living inter-connectivity, we each of us have had our time in the womb. We also know the struggle that is the passage of birth, and in this same way, we too can face every challenge; knowing that we do know how. We can all be the ones who birth new and creative solutions, restoring that same symbiotic harmony from inside the womb to outside of the womb, can we find those creative solutions from the living example of womb wisdom? From this direct experience of symbiosis, what if we actively seek to repeat this formula together. Why wait for a war or a crisis to come together, why not start right now?

When outside things appear not to be working, let us return inside, recalling our gnosis of being and discover our loving solutions from this space. If we feel angry or afraid, let us make time to do the work within rather than blaming another being. Now is the time to have courage, to make a stand for love, each of us in our own unique way. This will require us also to find the light, to plug into that power connecting us all to Creative Intelligence to take our visions into action. It is a divine 'hook up' that we all have to locate.

Every day, as part of a daily practice, I move and dance with music and then write; the words are written in a spontaneous flow of words that arrive uncensored onto the page. In this way, the words are coming from the soul or higher self, beyond the duality of the mind. I never change what has been written for it is an unedited flow of consciousness. This was a process that I was introduced to by Kim Rosen in her workshops. You can read about this in her book entitled; Saved by a Poem: The Transformative Power of Words. There are so many times when the words that arrive are direct messages from that loving field of intelligence, which lies way beyond the edited, critical and judging space of the Ego.

> **Inside my womb, the waves lap gently upon the shore,**

One after another in a rhythmic sequence that plays
Like a lullaby of sound, I hear the waves gently breaking,
upon all shores, the coming in and the going out,
a reminder of the one breath that fills us all,
so simply we breathe, never having to pause
for another breath arrives, it happens quite naturally.
In the same way that new life forms within the womb.
A sacred vessel of immense power and divine majesty
that cannot ever be taken away,
a birth right for each woman
to remember her beauty and strength
that lies within the potent lining of her womb.
The gateway through which every one of us arrives
A holy and sacred passage that is birth.

Chapter Two: CARIAD AND OUR TRUE STORY

Over many years, having the privilege to listen to thousands of stories shared, as a Counsellor, it has been evident that the one repeated cry from everyone that feels sad, hurt or lost in the world, is this idea of being disconnected in some way or another from love. We will all tell a different story but it will involve the notion that we are not good enough, or that we are to blame for the misfortunes of others. It is all my fault. Where do these ideas come from? For it is this story, that we are telling, and our habitual core beliefs, that are causing havoc in our lives. What we are so readily believing, it is all of these core beliefs that affect how we feel; both individually and collectively. These beliefs keep us separate from love.

Years ago, the world-renowned storyteller, Laura Sims, came to offer our community a workshop. Laura shared a story about one of the boy soldiers that she had met in Africa, how he had forgiven the boy soldier who had been responsible for murdering his family. How that boy was just like him, terrified and alone. In this madness they found solace in their own grief and here they both found connection.

Following this. as I shared a story, I had told so many times, regarding my own family and their loss of a baby girl, I realised that this no longer needed to be the narrative that defined my life. I wanted to become present, to see my own story as an opportunity for healing and not for perpetuating wounding. For I knew my Nan was 12 when her father was killed and she vividly described the issues that her mother faced. Then my mother lost her first child and again the same grief and torment filled their lives. There seemed to be no end to the eternal grief, when would they find joy again?

To find this joy would mean changing the narrative that had defined our lives. We could remain in grief, or make another choice. It took time to realise that if our life force is eternal, then we could choose to celebrate life rather than be lost in eternal grief, for we are all infinite love.

I know that there is relief in the knowledge that we are all infinite love and I chose to take this path. As the universe is always mirroring our own internal state, we must raise awareness of the type of person we want to be in the here and now. For it is in the awareness of our ego story that we realise we have another choice, to be our own compassionate witness, this will allow us to connect with love again and to be fully present. This will shift how we relate to ourselves and then to others.

We get to realise that these beliefs that we have taken up, have come from our own interpretation of how life was for us. This comes from our own individual mind. A learned interpretation of life, from others and the world at large. It is from here we have gathered all of these beliefs. From our parents, families, friends, teachers and society, the world around us; and just as I did, we can decide to shift our perception of our selves. We can choose love for ourselves which in turn shifts all of our relationships. When we can choose to be a reflection of harmony rather than discord, to allow love to flow, then we are tapping into our divine nature rather than our ego selves.

What we require, to fix our issues or our malaise, is to allow Love and Truth to surface again. We all have individual interpretations of the world, and they can feel very painful when we are lost in them. Yet, there seems to be one panacea that can cure all ills, and that is compassion. How does this link back to our consciousness? Well, our level of consciousness and the way that we view our world, and the people in our life, stems from the way that we feel about our own lives. Chances are if we feel we don't belong, this will produce a feeling of displeasure with life in general, it is coming from the feeling that we have generated within. I am unloved, others are unkind so the world then is not a safe place. These beliefs have taken us out of connection to love, and we separate ourselves.

For example, once I had noted my mother's apparent displeasure, aged 3, and believing that I was the cause of her upset, then my conclusion was that I was to blame. Of course, this was not true but as an innocent child, this is the feeling that I had internalised. Little did I know, having lost one child, my mother was always anxious. But instead, I became the culprit, and the cause of her unhappiness.

It seems reasonable from that moment on to try and please everyone, then if they are happy with me, then I can feel happy within myself. To do this, I am going to become the person I think others want to see, which is the end of me being my true and authentic self. However, now all the outer displeasure I perceive in my mother has been internalised. I am now stepping out of my authentic loving self, to be someone else. I have reinvented myself as a 'Pleaser' and this uses up lots of energy for I am living in fear. I just look up and see happy faces and believe that only if people are happy will I be safe. This of course is a mistaken belief; it is only me who has to change how I feel towards me. It is about being able to feel what arises within and let it flow. It is about reconnecting into the sense of joy, that existed within, before that event occurred. Because that sense of joy and the Truth of who I am remains unchanged by external events. Can you see how I have removed myself from the flow of life and stepped into a fear state?

It would follow that, if others were not happy, then I was at risk of being rejected by love again. In order to avoid the pain of re-experiencing rejection, it is vital that I am on top of how everyone feels. If I was to upset anyone then I could also get hurt. It was such a crazy notion; the world actually became a risky and dangerous place. On the other hand, prior to this event, I had felt loved unconditionally, and therefore, the world was a beautiful place and everyone, just like me, was caring and compassionate. Then it follows that our level of consciousness stems from how we feel about ourselves and the world we live in. It is an inside job. Reconnect with our inner joy and see it everywhere outside too!

With my second Grandson, as a baby, when I laughed or smiled his whole face lit up. It was only the expression of sheer joy that had an immediate response, is this because babies are wired for joy and pleasure? Is it true perhaps, that in childhood we all somehow separate ourselves from love and joy, not able to grasp that it lives within us, unchanged by external events?

There are also so many interpretations and views about love and life. Again, this will flow from our own core beliefs and the views, or opinions, that we form about ourselves and our life, all held within the mind. The good news is that the heart holds the Truth.

If we observe young children, we notice their inherent innocence in their connection to all of life. Following the flight of a bird, or watching an ant carrying a leaf, they are lost in the wonder and awe of life. They are not making interpretations with the mind, they are simply lost in the moment and caught up in the beauty of the world. They take each moment as it arises and live it fully, whether that be screaming for another drink to quell their thirst, or laughing out loud as the water splashes, in an unexpected puddle.

At what point does the spontaneity and the joy of life seem to evaporate? To be replaced with the careful weighing up of each moment, before making a reaction, or not speaking for fear of being wrong? It is well known that we formulated our core beliefs in childhood. From about the last four weeks before birth and up to around age seven; our brain is in a state of hypnosis, recording all that happens. Once the reasoning mind comes online with the prefrontal cortex, also around age seven, all these recordings become 'live' as our sense of self arrives. With the reasoning mind and all of its programmes now installed, whatever has been internalised as my sense of self, now has set patterns of behaviour. There is now a conditioned set of beliefs that are in charge of life, running the show, rather than the harmony and flow of love.

What happened in my own interpretation of events is that there was a separation. In the total innocence of the child, connected to the wonder of life, in that whole and complete oneness to all that is, there is an all-pervading connection that is unwritten and unseen for it just is. Like the web of a spider that covers the hedgerow, invisible to the naked eye. In an instant the connection may sever and break but only in my perception.

I froze, afraid that I had upset my mother, making her cross. What happened next is that now I am seeing myself as a bad person. The moment that I see myself as bad then I have separated away from love, believing myself to be unlovable. Now my opinion of myself is that I am a bad person. In the belief that I am not good enough to be loved then there is a shift, out of a direct experience of love through the heart, and into the mind as a set of beliefs is formed. It is this shift into the mind, to experience life as a direct result of how others value my behaviour, that has removed the sense of direct flow with life. Seeming to sever the connection to that all pervading web of life, the connection to oneness and love. But this has occurred in my mind as a direct result of my perception of events.

As previously stated, this is where my own core beliefs seemed to form. There is a shift from being free spirited, at one with all, to sensing my mother's displeasure and believing that I am the cause of her anger. Then in that instant, I am no longer innocent but casting myself as the bad person. The displeasure has been internalised on an unconscious level but it appears as disapproval of myself. We can all so easily step out of the connection of oneness. We can and all do separate from love, but this is because we have changed how we feel towards ourselves.

When we are in our heart flow with all of life, in love and perfect harmony we are a direct match for the 'hook up' to universal consciousness. However, once the love flow is interrupted, our perception of ourselves and life changes. It is almost as though the love circuitry is interrupted and we go into a default mode. Whatever occurs, it seems that the child holds themselves completely accountable. It is as though we sever ourselves from the source of life, which is love, and in that instant then, we are separate beings living in a mind story. From this unholy moment, where we have slipped from love, begins the narrative that becomes our life story, of separation from love.

What we must all recognise is that it is we who cut ourselves off. Somehow, we have slipped off the love radar. Maybe we do this for a good reason, to survive, but in cutting off this feeling, we somehow cut off from all feeling, not daring to feel again, or reconnect to the oneness, universal life force. We have lost the joy and spontaneity for we are now programmed by a belief system based upon fear.

Now we have become separate from the truth of consciousness and the divine harmony, that is all of life. Like Alice in Wonderland, we have fallen down the rabbit hole and we are faced with a set of Egoic and made-up beliefs that have caused a shift in our own felt sense of life, where we now see ourselves as bad. Just like Alice, nothing in our world now makes sense. There is a shift of consciousness, and it is only love that can pull us back out, for the truth is we are innocent, it is only by our own thinking that we are persecuted. What we need is love, to feel this within, for this is what connects us all in life.

Hatred, guilt and blame are held in the mind, (as our perception that we are no longer lovable) these are not holy instances that join and connect us as one, for they actually serve to cause separation from the truth which is love.

Those moments that do not connect us in love and joy, are going to be moments of our programmed story, of our mistaken beliefs. If only we can learn to look within for a more loving and truthful interpretation. What we need is to allow love back in, so that we can connect again, to feel and experience our own energy, the love and power within. For when we cut off, we erroneously seek all of that love power externally. We have to learn to live within our own skin and sense an internal resonance of love that connects us back into the universal field of source/love.

This looking within has been the work that has been developing over many years and now unfolds as the path within this book. CARIAD is a Welsh word that in translation means love or darling. It does not translate well into English as this word means so much more. When I watch my three-year-old grandson at play, there is love, he is a darling and at one with all of life. Cariad is such a beautiful word, and in searching for a name for the centre we will open, we knew this was the name for us. We have used this word for so many years, and living in Wales we hear the word, Cariad, so often spoken out loud.

It was two years ago that it became evident that Cariad was also spelling a solution, a path for us all to follow home to love. To become our own 'beloved' and connect back into the universal field of love that unites us all. From that consciousness of love, within us, we are free to be totally at peace and therefore we are always safe, and we will feel at home anywhere we live.

My son shared a dream he had recently, where he was trapped in a wicked world, that neither he nor his friends could escape. They were each trying to find the answer, to find the way out. It was finally a witch that told them, the only way out was to love themselves, only when they were love would they find the way out. Cariad is a sharing of the path into the love of self, this leads to a new life, an escape route from all of the pain and suffering. Do we need a witch to tell us or can we simply decide to begin connecting with love and our own innate wisdom? **There is no right or wrong way there is only love. CARIAD** actually spells out the following, it can be applied in all areas of life.

C - Compassion: with this in place we can feel deeply at peace, we feel safe and calm. We may have been connecting with 'self-hatred' rather than self-love, and we can search for the core beliefs that drive this response. No baby is born feeling unlovable, can we enable that journey back to love. opening to the truth that we are all infinite love.

A - Arousal: if we can learn to live with our emotions and feel at ease, we can allow intense emotions to rise and fall like the incoming tide, we will flow with whatever life brings our way. This occurs as we learn to understand our core beliefs and clear our conditioning, this allows peace and calm to resurface. We become aware of our emotional states and levels of frequency, then we can identify when we are out of alignment with the field of infinite love, and reclaim our rights to full power once again.

R - Reticular Activating System: that part of the brain that scans the environment and endeavours to match up our thinking and beliefs. We begin to fully grasp the principle 'as within, so without.' We can understand that a miracle occurs as we shift and develop a loving awareness of life, this frequency changes our own individual perception of our separation from life to reunite with the one consciousness of the infinite field of love.

I - Intuition: Within the left hemisphere of the brain is the logical, rational, linear thinking and the right brain is the seat of creativity and the home of imagination. As we relax and calm our inner state of being, we can learn to listen to the voice of our Intuition and follow our own higher guidance. We become aligned with our true nature, as infinite love; and in doing so we will be guided to follow a natural pattern that is pulsing through all of life. Universal consciousness.

A – Alignment, becoming attuned. With practice we will feel our coherence, as the nervous system of the body reaches homeostasis, and we have mastered the practices to be at one with our emotions and build resilience. We will feel the resonant collective field of Compassion that lives and breathes us all as creator conscious life-force.

D - Divine: Higher guidance is always available and the voice of our higher self leads us out of separation, then in the words of Ghandi; we will 'be the change we wish to see in the world'. And in the words of Richard Rudd, we will see the evolution of Homosapien to 'Homosanctus' DIVINE beings will emerge as we begin to recognise our true nature as a divinised being at one with the universal flow of life, which is love.

The Power of Love is Infinite, always flowing. We assume that we have the answers, but who is speaking? Who is it doing the talking? When I open my eyes to see, what do I see? Who is doing the looking? It is a practice, a spiritual one. to discern, to ask, as I did throughout my own life, 'How do I become a Clear Channel?'

'Simply Open', was the answer, 'And receive the Divine, for the Love is always flowing'…

The mind always seems to have a 'yes but' question, if I feel unworthy, what then? The answer: 'Impossible', for that is not an attribute of Source, unknown in the one infinite kingdom of Love. So how about 'Judging'? A slip into Ego, that's all it is. Staying awake, fully conscious, side steps judgments, they are of your mind, not that of Divine Creator Consciousness.

It is all about embracing simplicity, beyond the mindset that chooses to create an illusion of separation from love. Make time every day for stillness, give yourself over to peace, several times a day, listen for divine guidance and become present.

The invitation, before continuing to read, is to close our eyes, take a deep breath and ask for our own guidance, our Higher Self, to walk with us on this journey. Where are we all going? Into stillness and the peace within.

As you will see this is a path for reconnecting to the love that is the connection, the way and the Truth. It brings us all into inner harmony, as we reconnect to our innocence, then we are choosing to live in divine harmony with all of life.

If you choose you can take each step and simply read the description for each and contemplate and consider how this may unfold in your life. You may also like to delve deeper and connect for a more personal journey to look at your own life story, or indeed join a group with others also on this path.

Whatever you choose, I hope that you will enjoy reading and experiencing the CARIAD journey.

> **In these extraordinary times, let us remember all that is truth and be broken Taken beyond all limits of preconceived errors, to align with the custody of God's love and compassion.**

Chapter Three: COMPASSION

Pause here for a moment's reflection. Then read the next paragraph in bold, maybe even close your eyes and if you choose, you can place a hand over your heart. Simply allowing your mind to empty of all thoughts and arrive with a notion of being open.

Your truth is compassion, you are a sacred vessel of light and sound, beyond darkness. It is in receiving that you are given, as you feel you deserve. As you exchange your small will, for the open devotion of God's will, then all shall be open unto you; beyond all doubt and limitation. For love is the life-giving force that unites every being in holiness. It is in this truth, and in your sacredness, that you come fully alive; as this fills every cell in your body, your cup surely overflows. This is the destiny for every being to fill up and shine in full glory and radiance as a being of light.

If the underlying unmet need is always 'love'. There has to be a mistaken belief that separates us from love, like 'I don't matter' or 'I'm not good enough', 'I am unlovable' or 'bad things always happen to me'. These are mistaken beliefs, from our childhood and these are always keeping us separate from the missing ingredient which is **LOVE**. Once we can get that hug from Mum or Dad or a Grandparent, then we feel better. Why? Because this touch reminds us, and connects us, to that which lives within us too. With this feeling of love in place this supports healing, why? Because it reminds us that we are all whole and complete, which is why we feel better, for it is this love we most want to feel. What if this love lives inside of us all the time, in our cells, lying dormant, waiting for us to hook up to it once again? It does matter then that we are able to move past these beliefs that may be running our lives. We need to become present and assess how we feel now, allowing forgiveness, letting love in and accepting ourselves as we are now. Like a return to loving ourselves and accepting ourselves just the way we are.

We need to make time for heart currency to build up. With so many of the mothers, and even in my own life, it is evident that 'self-care' is always lacking. It is vital that mothers are supported, all of us have, what I term, an internal, 'love tank', and it needs to be replenished. We do this with small acts of kindness and for a new mother that may be as simple as even having time for a shower or a bath. This loving vital energy within is like a thermostat, it is regulating our loving heart vibration. When we make time and give to ourselves, the tank is filled once again. This is the same analogy as being on the plane and being instructed, as a mother, to be sure you fix your own oxygen mask first, before tending to infants. Quite obviously if we are drained, running on empty, how can we meet the needs of another. Depletion makes us cranky and out of sorts, that is why it takes a village to raise a child as every mother requires lots of nurturing support.

If it is love that underpins all of life, and this love is the essential ingredient for health, well-being and wholeness, how can we share more of it? After years of working and supporting others to heal, it would be fair to say that heart 'currency' is the real currency of life; for love is, almost always, the one panacea that heals all problems in life. I heard the term 'heart currency' for the first time from Sue Martin (read more about her work in Divine Design: Worlds Within Worlds).

I have found that if we can offer support, kindness and compassion, we can begin to breathe loving life back into hearts that have been held in loveless arms. We can all do this by seeing every person, on their healing journey as whole and complete. Maybe if we believe in their ability to find love within themselves, and offer the space for them to look inside, they will begin to feel their own strength and finally believe this once again. We create space for this healing when we see each person as an empowered human being and never as a victim.

As one of our group expressed, she found the path to loving herself so much easier knowing that all of us held her with unconditional love.

How do we truly learn to love ourselves? As we start our journey on the CARIAD path, in first learning to connect with love it is a good idea to empty our minds and come with a desire to be open. So simply let yourself be immersed in this journey into that connection and be open to what love can offer to us all.

We may begin by asking what we want for ourselves as we embark on this journey? How is it that I truly want to feel each day and what do I desire? What we, specifically, want to manifest, to bring into our lives, as we connect deeper into love and find our inner compassion.

What do we mean by the word compassion? Close your eyes, place your hand upon your heart and connect within, see when you look inside and ask this question, what comes to you then?

What I do notice is how difficult it seems for all of us to be compassionate to ourselves. How do we even cultivate compassion? For ourselves? For others and indeed for our planet?

If love can bring us together in that one consciousness, where we feel connected, how can we bring this into our lives every day? Many years ago, we were making a film about the work we were sharing in our community, and it was shared that being in our MAMs groups, mothers felt connected, they referred to this in their lives as 'the glue that joined the bricks'. Is this not the uniting effect of the love that binds us? Again, were they not tapping into this infinite field, 'when two or more gather', if our intention is love then this is felt by others; this is symbiosis, the feeling between all of us.

In the opening of your human heart, as the love (Universal love) flows, in and out, it flows through you. How about getting your stories, out of the way, for this field of energy to pass in and around and through you.

In simplicity, as you breathe in and out, empty the mind, focusing if you choose on joy, love and peace, whatever makes you smile, sigh and open further to love. You cannot get it wrong. Share this love with another and double yours. (Love yourself and Love your Neighbour as yourself).

Feel the beauty of our world, observe the bees in their creative endeavours, each bee is focused upon the union, the collective colony. The bee is not separate, it doesn't think I'll nick all the honey for myself! The bees work entirely together, in harmony, peacefully each bee goes about their own business, this is love-in-action; tuning into the colony, the needs of the whole and each one contributes to the hive. A hive of activity, all focused on the greatest good of all…they set us a very fine example to follow, look at all that they do; to serve nature, to create honey as a by-product of their harmonic convergence.

How could this be played out in our everyday lives? If each of us was serving the Divine Plan? To live in Divine Harmony, each of us with a pure heart, sharing our gifts and working together. There is enough food for the entire world so why should any human being die of starvation? Our role is to love, teach peace and to follow our hearts in open and complete connection.

There is a unity, a universal creative field of living, loving intelligence that ripens the apples from blossom to fruit, that hatches the chickens from their eggs and allows a mother to grow a baby in her own embryonic sac. All of this happens with no intervention from any of us. This living field can teach us all and show us how together in the same harmonic resonance as the bees, we can all exist together, we just have to tune in.

How is it that just as the blue flowers emerge on the Rosemary bush in my garden, the bees just all know the precise moment, that it is just perfect for them to collect pollen? How do all the animals, birds and insects know to move to higher ground as the Tsunami approaches? Or even my dog, as he wags his tail and makes a fuss, a full five minutes prior to the family arriving home?

Divine Universal Intelligence. You know when the phone rings and you know exactly who is calling. This Universal field of Intelligence is open in Divine Reverence. If we can hold within, this same resonance, the same loving state or vibration, then, I believe we tap right into this universal flow. We simply have to be open to receive, to relax, to flow and then we can tap into and follow this same loving intelligence, as it is eternally guiding us, bringing us home.

In the short story 'Wings of Love', that I wrote a few years ago, there are two small children and they rescue a baby from beneath the rubble. They escape their war-torn city ruins on the back of the winged horse, Pegasus. They may have witnessed violence, and seen acts of brutality, but what matters most, is that within their own hearts, they retain that open connection to the love that breathes them. They sustain that open two-way flow, to hear with the ears of Love, speak with the words of Love, and see with the eyes of Love. As Pegasus lifts them across the sky, it is an invitation to all of us to finally leave all of our old stories and our old wounding behind.

We are being invited to retain the essence of our pure heart always, and especially during times of adversity; to feel the force field of love that surrounds us and retain that level of awareness. At all times, to return to love, to feel how much we are loved; for each time that we share love and teach peace, we bring Salvation for all.

How then do we keep our light burning? How can we ensure that our own light keeps shining brightly? To ensure that our Consciousness is evolving.

Focus and make a commitment to keep awake and aware. What brings love to your life every day? We need to know this, maybe it is as you share in the beauty of nature or as you greet yourself in the mirror each day and say, 'I love you'.

It is up to each of us to do what brings us joy and to sustain this love within our open and pure hearts; from here we can extend that love out into our families and our communities, one relationship at a time.

Thinking about compassion. To be deeply loved and to feel truly loved, where and how do we learn to love? Surely love is the basic premise of life as in procreation, the founding principle. In all my years of being a Counsellor, this word, love has formed the basis of every session in some way or another. Either folks did not feel loved, or did not know how to give, or even receive love, and therefore, found relationships tricky.

I have had the privilege for many years to work with women in Refuge and those seeking support from traumatic family backgrounds. What was really noticeable was that most of us with these histories, had difficult stories entwined with the concept of love. When asking how much do you love yourself? The answer invariably was not very much, if at all. How sad that for so many of us, that feeling of being truly loved, was perceived as missing within the vocabulary of our human cells. Hence in that request to 'love your neighbour as yourself' that could look like the sharing of a self-hatred rather than a sharing of love.

Here is the very first principle of Cariad, as it all begins with Compassion, love at the root of life itself. However, I am fully aware that we do need to experience love and when I think of people who have openly shared love, I think of people like Nelson Mandela and Mother Theresa. There are also leading figures today like the Dalai Lama, and he openly shared that he attributes all that he is, to the love of his mother. There was also the life of Jesus, maybe we were not there to witness the miracles we read about; but we can, however, feel the gift that was his legacy, a transmission of love for us all, as a visceral way of life.

In the birth of a Cariad village, that is built with love at its core, then perhaps, together, we can all experience and share this love. I know first-hand that love is a gift and it flows, like a river through all of life when we can tap into this visceral source.

A few years ago, at my mother's bedside, following her stroke, I found myself in conversation with God. I was genuinely concerned that if she died then, she would not know how much I loved her. In that moment, on the threshold of life and death, all that mattered was love. It was important that I could tell her, so she knew how much I loved her. In that moment, I asked for forgiveness for all that had stood in the way of love for so many years. None of it mattered. The fact that my baby sister had died, and her life remained a secret, did that matter now? Of course not. Nothing mattered but love. What a sense of freedom rushes in when we do this. All of those hurt places just filled up with compassion and were brimming over with love instead of being blocked by pain.

As I sat there, deep in prayer, I watched the Blood Pressure monitor steadily drop and my mother slept peacefully for several hours. The next morning my mother was moved to a stroke ward with patients who could not speak, could not walk or even feed themselves. My Mother was left with deafness in one ear and after a few days rest in hospital, she was home, having made a full recovery.

Following that night in the hospital, I was able to take a short break. I found myself returning to the Chalice Well peace garden in Glastonbury, it was an opportunity to quietly give thanks for all that had occurred.

Resting in deep meditation and expressing huge gratitude that my mother was still in my life, feeling so immensely happy with the sun on my face, what happened next is not easily expressed in words. For suddenly my hand was taken and I was urged to follow a woman as she disappeared through a door and headed down a steep flight of stone steps. We were in an underground cavern, it was cold and the walls were wet, I was told to duck my head as I was pushed onto a boat that was passing through this underground waterway, I was hidden under a cover and told to be silent. From here, this figure took my hand and guided me along dimly lit stone passageways, up more stairs, all lit by candles, we hurried along until we abruptly stopped beside an open doorway on our right.

It was here that I was met with the brightest light that I have ever seen; it was blinding and far too bright to look into it directly. What I witnessed, from this doorway was a small cave-like room, with two women in the corner and one was clearly giving birth. Again, I was asked to remain silent, then this voice spoke to me, from within the light, it was a very profound experience and it felt as though I was in the presence of the Divine. I could just feel the extraordinary love and grace of this light, I was informed that what I was about to witness was a secret and then I heard very clearly, '**no one speaks about 'the Joy of Motherhood'.**

There was a profound message here, for not only was I training to be a Doula, but I already knew that my life's mission was to work with mothers. From here as I started to reflect that my mother had lost her first-born child and how their grief must have cut them off from joy. I was suddenly back in the garden where I started. It felt like just five minutes had passed but it was closer to an hour and my husband had been looking for me.

It was a profound experience that changed my life as I began to seek to understand, what was being shown to me. It was the recognition that this was the time now, to fully turn towards being of service. To see how it was possible to share this love more widely, with those who most needed to feel loved. Having spent many years, working with mothers, there have been many shared experiences of joy, most usually as a result of learning to forgive and let go of old patterns and stories that are no longer serving life.

The metaphor of birth also was very relevant in my own life, as with the letting go of life patterns and learning to forgive, a new compassion and energy for life re-surfaced and filled my own heart with joy. As Desmond Tutu shared in his 'Book of Joy',

'Forgiveness is the only way to heal ourselves and to be free from the past', and he goes on to say that when we cannot forgive the other person, they then hold the keys to our happiness and become our jailer. When we are able to forgive, we release our own pain and suffering, to restore the flow of the river as the compassion of life flows again.

What I have been shown, very clearly, as these visions continued for over a week, we can all make a difference, if we let love in. If we accept that we can open our hearts to love and then lead our children, by example. The ethos of Cariad is a community that applies compassion as a way of life, with the building of homes from sustainable materials. A community that makes a choice to live in harmony with one another and nature, here is where we can reconnect and feel this love flowing throughout all of our lives.

Let us all do the work to cultivate compassion, first within ourselves, then this flows to others and indeed out into our entire planet. We are the source of love that we seek.

If love can bring us together in that one consciousness, where we feel connected, how can we bring this into our lives every day? There is a quote by Rumi where he says:

'Out beyond ideas of right and wrong doing there is a field. I'll meet you there.'

What is this 'field'? Maybe what Rumi is hinting at here is the field of love, universal consciousness, that binds us all when we come into this place within ourselves. This same idea has been reflected day after day in the writing of poems and prose following my own morning practice of dance and contemplation.

> **It is in the undoing I'm done, emptied out, finished. Is this Surrender?**
> **In my heart, I'm home, in complete bliss, I rest.**

Sweet is the peace, Divine the unravelling, in one last push,
I'm arriving to greet myself, on this new day, a new dawn.
A beginning, Alpha and Omega, for I am back, where I began,
resting in the arms of love, here is the Truth of life

JOURNAL EXERCISE FOR COMPASSION

Explore in your own life where you feel love flows, make a note of how you feel. Like when we first fall in love. Or at the birth of a baby. Note how it feels within the body.

Conversely notice what happens when you feel anger or you get triggered, so then the love is no longer present, get curious, what are you thinking or believing? See if you can notice the feelings in the body, just be present to them.

Start a Gratitude list every day. Write at least 50 times I am grateful for… the bed I sleep in, running water, food to eat and clothes to wear etc.

Become present to your breath flowing in and out, sit in stillness and feel the breath. Relax and try some mindfulness practice or meditate. Or do some movement. This is all about getting present to the body in each moment.

Come into a gentle observation of all the feelings that flow through the body and notice when you are drawn out of a neutral stance of self-acceptance. Make a note of what you observe in your journal.

Chapter Four: AROUSAL

We have been bringing our attention to Compassion and now arrive at the letter A and the word Arousal as we begin to explore the feelings that reside within the human body. Can we notice when we are not in the experience of Love, Peace and Joy, what are the sensations that we are experiencing and how does it feel?

When we notice a feeling within, do we begin to tell ourselves a story? In our working with MAMs and our groups we wrote a programme entitled Changing the Story. It is an interactive programme that takes us on a journey to really feel into our own story. Perhaps it is about being aware of all the stories, we hear them every day. I recall two sisters, both telling the story about a family dinner that they had attended. They both sat at the same table and yet their versions of what they witnessed and experienced, were so entirely different, they almost came to blows. For each one insisted that their own version was correct. We see the world and experience it differently, and I am sure each of us has shared this same experience of viewing a situation in a way that differs from our peers or our own family.

I do wonder, when I hear so many stories, read them in the media and hear folks chatting as they are going about their business; how would it be if we could simply become present to what we feel, simply that; just give our awareness to our feelings. For it is our willingness to sit with these feelings, (and by bravely processing all of this) as we allow these feelings space to flow, then we can all reconnect into the power of love that unites us all. Instead of going into our heads and creating stories, based upon our past experiences.

Arousal is our body's felt experience of any given situation. What do we mean when we speak of our level of Arousal? Think of a time when you feel that you have been triggered. For when this occurs, we are in a reaction and you can be sure that we are no longer in the present, as a feeling is drawing our attention elsewhere. We could also talk about this in terms of our AWARENESS of our bodily experience. Being willing to be with the sensations of our body. Who is the one aware of the sensations? Who is the one listening and watching as life passes us by? Rumi talks of awareness in his poem The Guesthouse, and says that we get glimpses of this everyday as emotions arise within us. He calls them 'unexpected visitors', and at times when we are overcome with a sensation from nowhere it can feel like that. Where is the story we tell? What do we learn from our clan?

> *This being human is a Guesthouse every morning a new arrival*
>
> *A joy, a depression, a meanness, some momentary awareness comes As an unexpected visitor.*
>
> *Welcome and entertain them all! Even if they're a crowd of sorrows, who violently sweep your house empty of its furniture, still treat each guest honourably. He may be clearing you out for some new delight.*
>
> *The dark thought, the shame, the malice, meet them at the door laughing and invite them in.*

*Be grateful for whoever comes,
because each has been sent
as a guide from beyond.*

Jalaluddin Rumi, translation by Coleman Barks *(The Essential Rumi)*

This awareness of bodily sensation can be referred to as simply voltage, like a current of energy passing through us in a moment. On glimpsing a piece of striped shoelace, outside one morning, I froze, just for a second, was it a snake? Of course not, and then calm restores, but my body did react in a split second. So where does this 'inbuilt' reaction come from? I often tell the story of my son who is happy to remove spiders from the house. He simply picks them up in his hand and places them outside. Growing up with all of us afraid of spiders (as my mother and hers before her), it dawned on me that one child needed to have no fear to place spiders outside! This required making a huge effort to show no fear at all and capture many spiders in jars and place them outside, all the time shaking with the sight of 8 legs wriggling. I tried so hard to make sure that my fear was not witnessed, so could it be then that fear is something that we learn?

Anyone who has watched The Stillface Experiment, will recall how alarmed a young infant becomes, in less than one minute, when the expression, on the face of the mother, simply turns blank and expressionless. Why is this so alarming? She is still present and there, right in front of her child, but she stops playing and smiling, and her face goes blank and motionless. The child makes several attempts to get her to connect and then gets very upset. Why? Simply because the child wants connection, the child is observing, making sense of the world through his or her parents. I recall being sat on a passenger ferry and witnessing a toddler in a pushchair, one by one, every adult around this baby had become mesmerised by their mobile phone screens. I watched this baby move its eyes from person to person and then suddenly yell out! What was he feeling? Was it a connection that the child was seeking? If I had not observed my own mother's terror of house spiders, would I have been afraid? Is this because the child makes sense of the world by watching its caregivers? Monkey see and monkey do? What is your sense of this? Are you aware of what triggers a reaction in your body? Do you know the root cause of these triggers?

If we learn fear, then of course we also learn to love, by noticing how others care for us and respond to us when we are infants. We all do get a sense of awareness about how to react to our world from our parents and caregivers. Our neural chemistry, and brain wires, to adapt to the surroundings that we are placed in. Whether we are comfortable and calm, or anxious and stressed, how does this response arise within us? How is the nervous system reacting, calm or anxious? When do we learn to name it as a good or bad experience? I am only curious as over the years, I have noticed how stress does seem to be a learned response born out of our thinking with relation to the experience of our early childhood environment.

If we learn it, then it is also true that we can un- learn it as we grow our awareness. This requires of course that we first have to become aware of the sensations that we are holding. We can also notice if we feel restricted, a tightening or stiffness in our joints, these are messages that our body gives to us. We have expressions like 'that person is a pain in the neck' or 'that made me sick to the stomach'. We can name the areas of our body where sensation gathers. Are we tied and held up inside with fear and contraction or free with love and expansion? It would seem that how we observe the world and the impression that we perceive may impact our response to the way we feel? Or is it the other way around?

What I have noticed with many people, is that when they notice what makes them anxious, they are then aware of their responses. We can also pay attention to the way that we are breathing. This gives us a choice in any given moment, if I am not ok then I do have a choice to select a different response. Once we begin to be aware of our breath and how we are holding our body, even the thoughts that we are thinking, then we are becoming the master of our emotions. We can select how we wish to respond rather than our emotions running away with us. Fear is a natural response, if a bear is chasing us, it is wise to run, but if we are running away from feelings that are a reaction to events of the past, then the feelings have us, and we can now choose to shift our awareness and respond differently.

In becoming aware of how we feel and actively connecting with our bodily sensations, we then can impact the vibration that we are emitting. Entering a rugby stadium as the crowd rises and cheers their team scoring that winning try, we witness energy. The jubilation and exhilaration is tangible and we feel it, in the same way that we might sense sadness when we see a friend crying at the loss of their beloved pet dog. What you may not realise is that the vibration extends beyond your body. The

Heartmath Institute in America, tells us that the vibrational field of the human heart extends about 12 feet in front of us and all around the body, so as we move about, we encounter the heart fields of others. Ever felt a shudder or a sensation when in the company of another person?

You can also take a look at Hawkins scale of vibration, which indicates how various emotions resonate and are recorded at different levels. You can see Enlightenment, as we achieve that total bliss of being at 'one with all that is' and it measures at the top as 1000. Then you can drop to the other end of the scale and see Shame as the lowest vibration of just 20. But just like a drum beating, your heart resonance is sending a vibrational pattern out into the world. Are you aware of your own level of vibration? Are you aware of your heart rate variability, which is the space between the heart beats? There is a huge amount of intelligence within the human heart and here is where we need to place our attention.

To make a shift in our emotional state we need to be aware of how we feel. If we are feeling stressed and anxious then we can pay attention to our breath and see how we are breathing, noticing if our breath is short, and are we shallow breathing, from the top of our chest? Just by taking a deep breath into the body will shift how we feel. Try it, take in a deep breath right into the belly and sigh as you let it out. This deep exhalation says to the body, all is calm, all is well. Then we can slow it down and take deeper inhalations just paying attention to the rise and fall of the breath. By bringing our attention to our breath, and what we are thinking about, this will bring about a shift in our sensations. It is like our body senses we are aware and listening.

One of my greatest wishes was to have had greater awareness when raising my own family. As a mother, I had no real connection to my own volatile emotions, to have been taught emotionally literacy would have been life changing. It is our responsibility, as parents and grandparents, to manage our emotions so that we can be role models for our families. As my children read this they will roar with laughter, I was really blissfully unaware that the uprising voltage of my body could be managed. I am not proud to recall some of my crazy antics upon connecting with the big feelings in my own body.

It was many years later that the awareness developed regarding trapped emotions, and how these can be running the show. In a group training for Adlerian Counselling, we were asked can anyone connect to a memory from their childhood. Just as that thought registered, my legs began to shake uncontrollably and turned to jelly. I was holding onto my legs and totally bewildered, what was happening? Why was my whole body shaking? As I paid attention to the feeling, I drifted back into childhood and saw myself at 3 years of age. Here is an example of Arousal, the body is having a very big reaction, 40 years later! But the incredible realisation is that it was only my thinking and self-blame that was causing such a huge reaction.

Hence this writing, and sharing the path of Cariad, so that we can all now gather awareness as a community. In the sharing of this book and my work with parents, my greatest wish is for us all to continue raising awareness. It is down to us to become emotionally literate and make better choices in dealing with our own internal voltage. Rather than reacting and lashing out, can we take a pause and check inside? We could, for example, share our love and our resources, those small acts of kindness can shift the way that we view the world. The Cariad steps are widely shared within our Cariad Community. We plan to share them in our own Centre, here in Wales, a place for rest and recuperation, making time for ourselves to be still in our busy world. If we can share our resources and nurture both ourselves, and our land, then our world will feel like a better place for us all to live together in harmony.

A community that shares loving kindness can play a vital role in shifting perception as we have witnessed over the years with our MAMs Community Interest Company. When we receive that unconditional love, it allows us to pause and receive, this in turn cultivates an inner awareness that just, maybe, we are more than our human story and our human beliefs. It is from this vantage point that we may experience ourselves differently; and in turn our response to others will change. For if we do feel valued and loved, then we will share that loving kindness with others, but we need to first find this for ourselves. I am sure we all come into this world as divine and perfect beings and we need to remember this. It certainly was at the threshold of death that I experienced the full magnitude of the presence of God and from that moment onwards there was a wellspring of love that was always available. This flame, or spark of love, requires nurture, and a deep allowing, we need to get out of our own way for compassion to flourish and grow within.

Chapter Five: RETICULAR ACTIVATING SYSTEM (RAS)

Following through, with this chapter on the **RAS: Reticular Activating System**, we will recognise how **COMPASSION** for ourselves is really crucial. It really matters in our lives that we can be our own best friend and deeply care for ourselves. The journey is to become the beloved in our own lives, to move out of our headspace and enter the heart. As we soften and feel with the power and wisdom of the heart, this enables us to sit with big feelings and be able to tolerate our own states of **AROUSAL** without entering into story. We become our own Observer and witness how we are feeling. A chance to notice, have I moved out of the present moment? Which means now that my core beliefs are triggering a reaction. This gives us the evidence to say; this always happens to me, and here we go again, it can seem like Groundhog Day if we end up repeating the same patterns over and over. As the RAS is the filter in our brain, then by becoming aware of this, we can become co- creators of our reality, it matters, therefore, that we know how to use this to our advantage.

Now that we are raising our awareness as to the way that we feel, and gaining Emotional Mastery; we can explore this part of our brain known as the Reticular

Activating System. This small, little finger sized area at the back of your head, in the brain stem. It acts as a filter and as we cannot possibly process all of the information coming our way, it acts as a filter, to enable us to become more aware of where we place our attention for the RAS responds to what we focus upon.

To learn about the Reticular Activating System and how it functions, hands you the power to take charge of what you experience. Your own brain can support you if you realise that the RAS is a filter, in the back of the brain. It works through about 11 million bits of information per second that is being absorbed, in what you see and hear, taste, smell and touch. The brain can only process 50-100 bits per second, much of this is discarded as the RAS filters into awareness only that which is most important. What is it that you are choosing to focus upon at this moment? The job of the RAS is to filter out what you believe is not necessary and it does a thorough job. It sifts through all the information available, to present to you what matters. We need to be aware then, what we ask it to focus on, it will find what we seek. The RAS will select matches for your exact thoughts/beliefs. It will find all the evidence out there to support your core beliefs. If I have a core belief of 'I am not lovable', then 95% of what is happening in my world will show evidence to confirm this predominant thought I am thinking. Our thoughts are very powerful and creating what you are giving your attention to and showing it outside as proof that you are right!

> All the powers in the universe are already ours, it is us who have put our hands before our eyes and cry that it is dark.
>
> We are what our thoughts have made us, so take care about what you think. Words are secondary, thoughts live, they travel far.
>
> When an idea exclusively occupies the mind, it is transformed into an actual physical or mental state.
>
> We reap what we sow, we are the makers of our own fate. None else has the blame, none has the praise.
>
> There is no help for you outside of yourself, you are the creator of the universe. Like the silkworm, you have built a cocoon around yourself…burst out of your cocoon and come out as the beautiful butterfly, as the free soul.
>
> Then you alone will see Truth.

In one word, this ideal is that you are divine, God sits in the temple of every human body.
Vivekananda

Can we pick up the judgments that we make upon ourselves, for example, I'm useless, no point in my self-expression as no one is listening or cares, they don't love me etc. All these beliefs might mean that I develop a coping mechanism for life, and perhaps I decide to hide away, to not talk and live in my own imaginary world. Then begins the story, where I see that I am separate from this world, and not part of the whole. In this instance, you are in your own bubble and cut off from 'flow' or from the source of all power, which is love. There is a problem with these coping strategies in so much as we remain stuck in these old patterns and worn-out beliefs. Also disconnected from our joy and pleasure,

As you begin to realise that we all live in a benevolent and loving world, it may begin to enter into your awareness that love connects us and fear separates us. Then you can see how the RAS really brings in the experiences that we need to grow and to shift from fear to love. In these words, from Vivekananda, we can see that 'we reap what we sow'. If we remain unconscious, which we can choose to do, are we in fact giving away our power?

What if we make a choice to gain a conscious understanding of how we are using our own brain filtering system. We do this each time we feel our own voltage, let it be, and accept ourselves and our feelings with love. From this vantage point we can now see, if we know this feeling, and have we felt this before? This may allow us to gain an awareness of a time, or situation in childhood, maybe where there is some unfinished business. Big feelings that are simply needing to be allowed space to move through.

When we take a pause and look within, we create space. This spaciousness allows for an expanded awareness to develop. Rather than just seeing inches in front, we travel up to ten thousand feet and view our life experience from here. We often noticed, in our MAMs groups, that during the first week, we heard stories and people seemed trapped in them. By the last week, they all had their same stories, but they viewed themselves and their experiences with love rather than with fear. It was their consciousness that had expanded, and so let more light within.

How often do people share their fears around tests and exams? Maybe they meet the full force of 'you must succeed,' unable to even look at, or feel, what to fail could mean. Here is the false belief of my worth is tied up with success. I have already shared the pleaser's fear of rejection. False beliefs, or mistaken notions for truly, if we sense we are being externally 'got at', the chances are, we are already attacking or judging ourselves on the inside. How could I be so stupid. I should have known better. I get the blame for everything. No one cares what I think anyway. I am invisible, I may as well not bother. Take a breath, relax and place your hand on your heart, check in from here, are these beliefs true?

Overall, we have lived in times of Patriarchy and before that Matriarchy and now we are finding the balance in between the two. Finding a new era emerging of Love, Joy and Peace. Finding this within ourselves, this balance and inner harmony, becoming aware, that the RAS is our filter and it is bringing into our lives, that which we focus upon!

What we can do is to ask ourselves, how do we find this calm and peace within? We can begin by learning to sit and feel, learn to be with those volatile emotions arising. Fear is Frozen Energy Awaiting Release, or another acronym for fear is, False Evidence Appearing Real, whichever you choose, this is the vibration of our most sacred wound. Here is where we get to stay present to this energy arising within and enable this power to be harnessed for our growth. So, when we feel all the energy rise straight up, as those buttons get a direct hit, we need to get better at owning this energy rather than pushing it away.

Owning these buttons, gives us a chance to feel how we feel, to get curious about the first time I felt like this, or when I first started to blame myself or become judgmental and critical of others? By exploring our childhoods, how were we nurtured, what were our early childhood experiences? For what kinds of behaviours did we get noticed? Were we being the most and best well-behaved child in the land, how did you get rewarded? Chances are you will still do this or your family will still remind you. Mine was the pat on the head, closely followed by cake or sweets, so I still reward myself with chocolate! We do learn to conform in childhood, but now we are bursting out of the cocoon of this self-imposed safety zone and it can feel uncomfortable, right?

Become aware of your patterns and habitual responses as these are being fed into the RAS, and in doing so, your experiences are being filtered to create the reality of your choice. You might explore what brings calm and peace, what brings you into a place of neutral or feeling a sense of I am OK. Notice what works for you and do more of it, dance and sing, dig and get into nature, whatever does it for you, do ten times more of that this week! Watch the reset happen within, as you allow the RAS to filter in what you want to experience.

The old ways are no longer working and redundant; you are the ones who will get curious and ponder long enough, to be creative in finding new solutions. To bring in new ways of being more and doing less, as we create a world anew from the inside. It is interesting to recall Einstein's quote; 'no problem can be solved from the Consciousness that created it'. Emotional Mastery combined with a heart-focused approach, allows you to BECOME THE CHANGE YOU WISH TO SEE IN THE WORLD. Breaking away from me against the world and embracing, together is better, for we are all part of the whole. Sharing and caring while feeling the new currency of life which is LOVE: Cariad Connect, feel it inside and take it out into the world

If I focus instead on, **I am love and every day my life is filled with loving experiences**, then this is what I am going to notice. Why not try this for yourselves? Focus on what you want to experience. What you most desire. When we can enter our hearts and create from here, which is where we find peace, then we can hear the voice of wisdom. Intuition is that voice that speaks softly and quietly waiting for us to listen. From the poem Deep Listening, by Rumi this line is one of the best to describe this: '*I should sell my tongue and buy a thousand ears when that one steps near and begins to speak*'

Homework: If you have not yet set an Intention, for yourself, try and set one each week, or daily perhaps. See this as an opportunity to test your RAS, to provide evidence and draw to you what you are wanting to experience.

> In my heart is love, a transmission for my cells, a community of 50 trillion cells that fill my body. Each one has a receptor picking up signals, how am I feeling? What message do I convey in my thoughts and perception of life?
>
> Am I safe and happy, fulfilled and at peace? Or feeling threatened, unworthy and tormented? Truth is my cells cannot see beyond the boundary of my skin. They simply lay their trust in me. Am I a fearless, heart strong warrior or am I weak, worried, lost and feeling like a victim? The truth is I am creating an environment internally that is reflected in my outer world.;

My cells are only responding for each thought is producing bio-chemistry on the inside.

I feel responsible to convey the right messages, to ensure that I am telling the Truth and perceiving the full picture. I'm creating a film, where I play the main Character and Director, so I am scripting carefully, choosing thoughts that convey the Truth, ones that enhance life, ones that inspire love and right action, in that way I am caretaking my cell community to fully converse with the beauty of life…

Chapter Six: INTUITION

Where do we gather our inspiration from? It is interesting when we listen, what is the voice we hear, that speaks to us, that guides us and prompts us to take a left instead of a right turn. When poems and words arrive, there are times when I am left baffled and need to go and find out what certain words mean. This is a sure sign that this flows from beyond my own awareness. If it is my Ego, or conditioned mind, that speaks, more often than not, it is judgmental or critical, probably because the seat of awareness is my own mind, a storehouse of all of my previous experiences. These days, it is the universal or Divine Creator Consciousness that is my go-to for inspiration, where my heart opens and life is joyful. Then the seat of my awareness is with my Higher Self. A greater sense of Awareness inspires creativity and love in action. A preferred state to that of being locked in with all my past experiences and going round in ever decreasing circles getting nowhere.

There is a clue in the word 'in-spire', from the origin of this word, meaning 'to breathe or blow into, often from a divine being, to impart a truth or an idea.' When we follow this quiet voice, this is our higher self or our soul speaking, it is very different to the critical voice of the Ego.

Have you ever noticed when you lose track of time, and you are so in the moment, that answers to questions seem to come from nowhere? This is the intuition dropping in for us, as we are learning Consciousness Control and Mastery of Emotions/Energy, the voice of wisdom can be heard beyond our own prevailing thoughts. We also need to note that at the times that we lose track of time it is because we are present.

Thinking about the opening of this book, we looked at the expression from the bible 'I AM/ You are the light of the universe', it is Eckhart Tolle who sees that the word, light, is actually Consciousness. We have started to see how we can learn Conscious Control and Mastery of Energy. In this way, we are looking at IN-TUITION, we are going within and being our own Teacher. When I am more than my emotions, there is room for expansion. We are once again, following the wisdom and intuition coming from the flow state of being connected to Source.

We are all born with this connection open, and children directly connect, which is why they are so 'in the moment' as they follow this spontaneity and see only love and beauty all around. How would it be if we were able to be so innocent again in the way that we see the world? As we turn seven and learn 'this is a tree', and' this is a house', then we begin to place labels upon things and definitions that have been given to us by others. Perhaps in our homes and in education, for our culture is our source of information, this gets stored within us and we then lose sight of our own direct connection and turn to the mind for our answers. So, nothing fresh is arriving if our 'go to' is stored memories.

We are all now taking time for in-tuition, that inward journey to self-mastery, which means we are going into the stillness to RE-CONNECT to source once again, to increase the light that flows through the cells of the human body as more consciousness transcends, we are aware of the oneness. Once this occurs, we move out of the mind, with the trapped thinking of this is right/wrong, good or bad. We move beyond the duality of the brain to a place where we can view others and the world with no judgment, here is our heart connection.

In all the groups and individual sessions that I have had the privilege to offer, I have noticed how there is often a pattern to defend and attack. You probably have witnessed yourself or another, become triggered and lash back or have a big reaction. It is possible to go from calm to very angry in half a second. Why is this? Calm one minute and then very upset, this is how powerful the mind can be when we access a connection to a memory of the past. Core beliefs come out to be felt and expressed. Ever noticed how tiring this can be? To be so angry or upset, it can be exhausting, and with good reason, because energy goes where we place our attention.

What is it that causes the upset? It may be, for example, the belief that 'I am not lovable', it was certainly my own childhood belief. To explore this, in terms of love and energy, when someone becomes very angry, in the child's world, the angry reaction represents the withdrawal of love. You are angry, not happy now, and so I am the cause, so I must be bad. To feel this is huge for a child, that feeling is almost unbearable, that love is not there for me, if it gets repeated, many times, then this can become a behaviour pattern. In this case, my mistaken belief is that if I am bad, love gets withdrawn. <u>Guess what, I spent a lifetime avoiding the rejection of love, all because I did not want to feel this love withdrawal.</u>

It is bad enough to feel this once, but to go on believing this, avoiding rejection, it is so tiring. There is a need to defend and attack all the time, but it is me who ends up exhausted and fed up, because I am always waiting for the next assault to occur because I am unlovable and I can collect lots of evidence for that all day long! What is it that I am needing? It would seem that the perceived unmet need is love. A hug, some attention from someone to say that they care, this is reassurance that will say to me that it is ok, now I am ok, because someone loves me. Inside my nervous system calms down. Phew, that pattern is taking a whole lot of energy. What if this is not true? What if love was never withdrawn, it was a mistaken belief, faulty thinking of a small child. The saving grace is to really begin to question the truth and validity of these beliefs, is it true, really true, that I am not lovable? Of course, it is not true, it is only my Ego or childhood belief. The real big shift came when I began to realise that I am loved, simply because I breathe, that the love was never taken away or withdrawn. It helps to have faith and know that there is a greater presence in the world than just little me. This enables perception to shift out of the stuck pattern of self-blame and into self-love and expansion.

To delve deeper into this there is a Process called 'Six Steps to Freedom', that expands in more detail this methodology for questioning our childhood beliefs. Diederik Wolsak's book 'Choose Again' provides the details of the method. This is precisely the lynch pin of this whole process. I get to choose again, if I am not experiencing peace, now as an adult, there is the opportunity to choose something different, and I am in charge of how I feel, no one else. In this way, the love comes back inside of me, and I really get to understand that love is constant all the time and the Truth is, it never left.

Children are born with this ability, living open-hearted, they can teach us how to move beyond all of our fear-based beliefs and become aware of our constant connection to the universal field of love/oneness. What part of ourselves gets hidden away when we self-protect, or hide away because we do not trust others? It is this beautiful loving essence that is the very core of our being Our Life's Work, is really to look at how we separate from love and step back fully into our true authenticity.

We all could be exploring heart currency, what is it that brings us fully alive and opens our hearts in full connection to Source. Then there could be a shift from just selecting a job for money, to really exploring, what is my unique gift that I would like to share with the world? The irony is when we do what we love, we will live life and be happy, plus at the same time, we will earn money. When we flow from authenticity, we also experience health and well-being for we are flowing with creation, we live in abundance.

How do we move fully into this expression of our true authenticity? Where we get to tap fully our divine essence then our own, USP, Unique Self-Potential can come online as we share our Gifts. Each person being truly authentic so that we can be the change that we want to see in the world. In my own case, there was a driving desire to become, emotionally literate, and share that with other mothers so that both they, and their families. could live happily and peacefully together. When we discover that love lives inside of us, this creates an opening, and in my case, the freedom to love and respect myself, and live life fully, in peace and joy. I am sharing that which I really needed to learn and at the same time earning a living.

Now every day is a joy and repeatedly those around will hear me say: 'I love my job!'. For this to happen, there had to be a huge shift from, seeing a job as a means to an end, and a supply of money, to really living my life in its fullest expression. And what led me to this path was finally being still enough to hear the voice of my intuition. Sitting in meditation, my higher self, my own inner guide, is suggesting that I need to text a colleague, and offer my services to support others. I did this, and as a result of the telephone call that ensued, I began to offer my services as a Counsellor and a whole project developed from this one text. Remember, I had not left my seat, nor gone to look or search for it, there it was, I simply followed my intuition.

A starting place for turning inward, is learning how to become more present / in the moment and this is where you start to notice what brings joy and peace into your daily life? Already, we have looked at the breath, we can also become more attuned to our Intuition by connecting with nature. What is it that you are doing when you become aware that you have lost all track of time? Or what is it that you simply love to do, just because you can, for yourself? Make a list and use it to remind yourself. Over the years we have collected quite a list, what can you add to these suggestions?

In relaxation, walks in nature, meditation and stillness, mindfulness, yoga or tai chi or dancing, breath, doing what we love, gratitude attitude, prayer, contemplation, swimming in the ocean. Communing with nature, singing, movement, pets and animals, poetry, chanting, painting and mantras. Please add more to this list.

Once we can connect to this peace within, then the doorway to our higher self or our own inner guide is pushed open. In those quiet and calm moments, we can be present and feel into the right decision by noticing what feels right for us and listening out for the voice of our intuition.

We may have an ongoing problem for which we can now find a solution, the answer often comes through from an expanded level of Consciousness. You are your best inner tutor, lean into your life and let the love and energy flow in the moment and be open, be curious and see what happens.

Other steps that help, ask a direct question. With the story above, what paved the way was asking for what I wanted. I had asked out loud: 'ok I am happy to work and support others, what is the next best step that I can take?' We have to be clear, recall how the RAS works, we need to ask for what we need. You can also set an intention and repeat it several times: 'I am happily working, doing what I love and all of my bills are covered.' Then see what guidance or signs you get.

> **There is an interior peace within my being, where lies a Truth, coiled deep in my cells. Such a mighty presence, a governing vessel, that bequeaths all requests from a visceral, heart-centred knowing, we are all this and so much more, resting in the Gnosis.**
> **A wisdom of an internal universe just below the surface.**
> **Wide sprung coils send out signals of electric, pulsing to return our desires;**

heaving on impulse and gifted back in our field of vision...

Chapter Seven: ALIGNMENT

What is Alignment, and how do we know, or more importantly how does it feel when we are aligned? We spoke about the baby in the womb in a symbiotic relationship with its mother, it is my belief that we enter this world in that same symbiotic connected state of being. Attuned with all of nature and at one with the universal flow of life. It is this connection to the energy that we need to feel, to allow the life force to fully flow within our bodies. When we are a full resounding YES to the energy within our bodies then we are in alignment. We are tapping into the loving power that is life and letting it flow through us as though we are one with it, because we really are all of this!

There are many of us sensing a struggle at this time, it is almost like the witch dream that my son shared. They were all flying around and feeling all of their old stories and old emotions that were just keeping them trapped. It was exhausting, the witch informed them that they would all be stuck there until they learned to love themselves. Once they filled up with love then they were free and they could fly off and they were no longer trapped. Where are you feeling trapped by your own stories that are keeping you stuck and preventing you from aligning to love?

At my mother's bedside, I totally aligned with love, and released all my old stories. This felt like such a release and in truth it was exhilarating, my body had a new lease of life! The reason for this is explained by Richard Rudd in his book: Gene Keys. When looking at the shadow of Universal Love, he notes: 'How fear creates its own biofeedback loop, which maintains the constriction of life force inside you'. This is so true, each person that moves out of fear and into a more loving acceptance of themselves, experiences this surge of vitality, like a huge YES to life. No more hiding in fear, we feel it to heal it.

We all need to be finding this internal alignment with love for externally, in the world, we are capable of literally birthing a new way of life, a new way of being in the world and our bodies. Right now, it is possible to make this switch as even our DNA is re-structuring and realigning to this state of oneness. Sensing and connecting to harmony within to enable us to feel that outer peace in the world that we all share together.

In my experience of working, I can only say that when we reach an inner alignment and peace then it is reflected in our external world. With everyone that says they feel anxious, I always invite them to put a hand on their heart and breathe steadily in and out. If they pay attention to their breath, and place their attention on the heart, they shift focus out of the thinking mind. This always brings in an almost instant sense of calm. We need to get used to feeling when we are aligned, and in a flow state, or out of it. Most of us seem to sense when we get out of bed on the wrong side, and stub our toe, and then the day goes from bad to worse. We also can feel when we are loving life and at peace. Most of us have no problem with expressing how we feel. and we equally all know, when we feel ready to explode! Explosions in the emotion's factory! It is at these times that the call is to go within and to feel, we may want to shake or dance or scream and move, but whatever we do, it requires that we feel the voltage of emotion arising within, and simply be present. We need to learn to be with our emotions, rather than shoving them onto someone else, or blaming another person for the way that we are feeling. You know how this works; we have all lost it at some time or another. But it is no longer acceptable to use others as a dumping ground for our feelings.

Once we can learn to be with our feelings, using our breath, sounds or moving, then as we discussed we start to get our inner awareness working. We can connect then to our Intuition; with practice this gives us a sense of a bigger power beyond our little Ego self. We feel connected to the entire universe, then it is far easier to 'get out of our own way,' we can sense the universal intelligence that is there to support us and hear the voice of wisdom that is there to guide us. How often though do we block this? We cannot hear our inner voice of wisdom if we are afraid or in a state of panic. Also, we shared that we do need to become present and, in the moment, to sense or be intuitive. Anxiety shows us that we are out of alignment and in a story. A time to let the SHIT (Stories and History Interfering Today) all go. We do get to choose how we feel moment to moment. Remember, it is a choice. I found the acronym works because it is all Stories and Core Beliefs and they get in the way of us living life to the full and connecting to the vitality of life lived in true authenticity. I get to choose how I feel and connect to love and joy.

For when we are really present, attuned and in flow, this is where we will feel our heart opening, and we naturally will make the best choices for ourselves and others. It is from the heart, that we are in fact selfless, tapping into universal consciousness. Which is different, as we discussed from connections that come from our beliefs or the conditioned mind, which is just full of all of our past stories. For in this state of mind, the power leaves us as we desire to possess or have attraction to form outside of ourselves. This is all about the small personality which makes choices based upon past beliefs and past experiences. There is a difference between those decisions from an Ego perspective to those that we make from the Truth of our being. For when we are in alignment with all that is, here is the unconditional love, where we remain unchangeably innocent, whole and complete. The heart awakened state rather than the closed heart state of being.

How do we suspend all egoic drives to feel that alignment to universal love, which is all that there is when we get beyond our small human selves? I know that this was my own personal experience when my mother was close to death, once I surrendered my own egoic nature and chose to release all stories and forgive all that had gone before, I spent a week in this glorious field of divine love and flow, feeling connected to all of nature and every being. From this place it was very clear that this universal loving intelligence is all that there is and it is blocked out by our all fears and judgments.

It has taken a further four years to fully grasp the magnificence of what happened and to truly comprehend or even try to make sense of what took place. Yet, as I write this it is clear that this is a visceral gnosis, not a concept grasped by the mind. But I am sure that each person has their own experience of a time or place where they have felt this loving intelligence. There are times when I do feel that Divine Consciousness is indeed breathing my body and I feel part of this living organism. It seems that we are being guided to trust this divine intelligence and universal flow and re-align to this presence. How we each do this will be different and we need to become aware, when we feel the flow, or notice what we are doing and how we are being when this happens? This allows us to notice what is enabling us to lighten the load, lose our emotional density and become that clear channel. You will notice the shift of energy is uplifting, it is easy and you simply feel at peace, like living in a state of Grace.

It is true that we are all learning, all of the time, and in this work, I am trusting my own flow and sharing **Cariad Connect**. We know that it is time for new ideas and therefore it is vital that we let our own creativity flow. It was not always easy for me to trust this flow, I did compromise many times and in doing so, found myself off the path and out of Alignment. I tried to tick the boxes for what others wanted, or expected, and in doing so all the time I was ignoring my own divine wisdom. You see the learned 'pleasing' behaviour that I adopted out of fear would have me please everyone externally and negate myself. I was actually afraid to talk openly about 'love' and bringing this into our work environment. Yet as soon as I listened within, and followed my own true nature, then it provided the impetus to begin to share **Cariad Connect**. It did feel uncomfortable. and the exposure of my own writing, brought up old patterns of self-doubt. Nonetheless it was time to push through, so here it is, and in some ways, perhaps it will serve to inspire others, to trust their Intuition and their own Inner Wisdom. For if we connect to our hearts, following the inner journey, then imagine how our world might look, if all learn to change our outer reality.

There is a re-wiring that takes place in the brain and for me there was a huge shift. I no longer was trying to keep everyone on the outside happy to find peace within. Now I was finding the peace within and following that flow towards external action, it was a complete transformation to feel comfortable within my own skin first. After all, if we are feeling uncomfortable within our own skin then the chances are we have been ignoring how we feel inside and trying to just please everyone on the outside and it does not work. Seek out, instead, what it is that you truly desire and be aware how you want to feel every day. It is an inside job; I have followed the natural impulse to reconnect to the source of life, and so can you.

Let this wash over and embrace your heart, feel each note resonate as a vibration, A sound that

unites us all in this moment where you glide effortlessly, needing nothing. You can be emptied onto a vast galaxy of ever-present joyous celebration and laughter. Cherish the pauses and spaces, lean into heartfulness, awe and wonder for they are the cornerstones of this experience, cells uplifted, cherish this feeling. Inhale the essence of Divinity and be intoxicated, swept away into rapturous chords of resonant sounds that echo in all the chambers of the heart. Electrifying and recharging batteries so life force channels the current of one love, one life, one people. There is nothing here but love, joy and pure bliss. Breathe in the essence of love. transcend, sit by the waters, bathe in the heavenly blue mists and rose oils. See the purple iris growing by the water's edge, swim, be immersed in the waters and float as the lily does.

This is my Life's Work, and if you want to get an idea, or use the 'cheat sheet', you can check out your Life's Purpose through Richard Rudd's work and Gene Keys. You will need your date, time and place of birth, then you can find your life path and your Life's Purpose Gene Key. Embracing your higher purpose, this is related to astrological data via the I Ching, so you can understand the evolutionary flow for yourself. We are invited to find the Gift within our Shadow, the aspects of ourselves that are so often hidden, or the ones that we want to avoid. But in the shadow lies our higher purpose, when we look at this and become aware of what we are finding most difficult or what is really hard for us; this is exactly where we need to look. The shadow that I had to overcome was Compromise, but we need to find our own struggle and embrace it. This is where we need to look inside of ourselves and search within to see how this shadow operates. The reason we must all search inwards into the shadow realm, is so aptly expressed by Etty Hilliesem, in her Diary Extracts:

'Each of us must turn inwards and destroy in ourselves, all that we think we ought to destroy in others and remember that every atom of hate we add to the world makes it still more inhospitable'

Etty, died in Auschwitz, just before her 30th birthday, you can find this quote in her book, An Interrupted Life.

Once we can embrace the shadow, we will locate the gift, which in my case brought the creativity to connect and create relationships, then the next level after the gift, is the siddhi which brings you into connection with the unified state. All of this is encoded within your DNA as this is your root to the unified state and your style for getting there is unique to you. Our highest or Siddhi state unlocks our genius, the genie in the bottle! The website link is here: Genekeyprofile.com

Homework: Explore how you find your flow. Are you truly aligned with your passion? The best way to dream our future is to hold a really big vision, mine is that **'every child will rest in love'** and what will yours be? How can I be of greatest service to the whole? Try repeating this question and see if you get any answers. If you do look up your Gene Keys then you can get to know your Life's Work if you choose to.

Chapter Eight: THE DIVINE WITHIN US

What do we mean when we look at the 'divine' within us? My own interpretation is that this manifests as our internal state once we become a clear channel. Literally, this will mean that we have cleaned up all our old beliefs and patterns and got out of our own way. We then stop 'reacting' to big feelings and looking externally for the cause of our pain. Instead, we are connecting to our emotions within and allowing them to pass through us. Like voltage that fires up the battery, these emotions become a source of power, rather than something that destroys us. Like the Phoenix that rises from the ashes we are using the fire of our emotional being to transcend the set patterns of stored experiences. We are then riding the crest of the wave, in flow, rather than being battered inside and dragged along by the current. Once we achieve this, it is like the 'force is with us', we are tapping into the universal force field that breathes life into every being.

This was my own experience by my mother's bedside, following her stroke. Once I released and let go every single belief and pattern that I held within, I simply became a clear channel. Without any conscious awareness, but in love and by holding absolute forgiveness for myself, for all previous beliefs; this released and transformed my state of being into flow consciousness. This experience lasted for about seven days, or until, I believe, I dropped out of that state of unity consciousness. What happened in those seven days was that I seemed to be able to slip behind the veil of my illusory self, the one with old belief patterns. It was as though in a state of being one with the divine; it was only possible to witness others with the same unity consciousness, speak to them, and hear their voices as this too.

It was a mystical and magical experience, that words cannot even begin to explain, but I do believe that I may have experienced what it is to be a 'Clear Channel' at one with the Divine. Throughout those seven days it was like being in a state of bliss and complete connection to all that exists. Since then, it has been a question of finding the resources, and the know-how, to try and give form to this experience, as a path to guide others who may choose to follow. What is apparent, is that it is by raising our vibration and transmuting all of our own shadow consciousness this is how we evolve and grow.

We explored in the last chapter around this idea of ALIGNMENT, how do we begin to find and locate this state of being? Many people have shared their own stories, suffice it to say, there can be a lot of stuff emerging for all of us, as we begin to delve deeper, to know thy own true self. It is to be expected, as we are really becoming conscious, to our own internal process, that we will notice our feelings more. We are witnessing our own emotions and feeling into those waves arising, noticing this in ourselves and in others too. Of course, it is tempting to look outside and say 'oh it is because... they said this or did that'. However, we are wise enough now, to look a little deeper, and search for the answer from within, feel the velocity and accept it, allowing it to pass through. Right? I know that this is not always the case, trust me, it is not that simple and the waves always keep coming, we just need to get better at surfing them. I am learning to keep surfing those waves, every day!

We can stay in defence mode and feel the cost of resistance when we are not riding those waves, we are getting lost in a sea of emotions and pulled under! It has been a tough time for many with a worldwide Pandemic, and if, like me, you lost your surfboard, that's perfectly natural. The main reason that we need to be really aware of what we are cooking on the inside, is because this impacts our vibration or state of resonance. Look further at the Hawkins Scale of Consciousness for more details on the levels of vibration and his scale. As we read earlier, Dr David Hawkins devised a scale with shame as the lowest vibration right up to joy and unity consciousness or enlightenment! It pays to be aware then of what lights you up and what dampens your frequency. Because outwardly, what is showing up in our lives, is a match for our internal state of being. To evolve is to be aware. To know what is active within our own sub-conscious as well as the collective subconscious of humanity.

In my own journey, as I have shared, it has been about rising into Sovereignty, a journey to overcome my own self-doubt. Previously not believing in myself led to so much compromise, trying to fit into what other people felt was right, or not having the confidence to follow my own path. Now as I have stepped into trusting the Divine, it feels as though I have reached a level of competence. Which has led to following that Divine Inspiration that manifests as 'love in action' and the publication of Cariad.

You see when we can dwell in the shadow, it is this very struggle that lifts us through discovering the gift that it holds for us, we have to learn to be in the world as love itself. Perhaps it is this inward struggle that we are all feeling, being mirrored externally in our world outside? What if it is perfectly natural, as we all evolve and grow. We will witness the end the Piscean Age, this needs to occur, we need to rise up from our own shadows and birth this new paradigm and the 'Age of Aquarius'. There has already been a huge shift for humanity. It helps to be aware that there is a shift occurring, which means that more of us will make it through the struggles of the shadows and in doing so, we will be born again into a new frequency and new experiences. If we can be still, and trust in the chaos around us, then we will switch from fear into love and connect to the benevolence that truly is awaiting us all in the beautiful planet that we all share together. We are reminded that this is the time for following our own natural guidance and evolving beyond our old patterns of behaviour.

When others have taken this path, they have found that they reach a flow frequency, being aligned with their true loving nature, and so their outer world does shift. We awake from the illusion. For some it has been that they find the perfect job, or they feel better about their partner and happier in their relationships, find love with a new partner or re-connect with loved ones, what each person knows, without doubt, is that they are the source of their own happiness. They do not enter a relationship as 'needy' with an expectation that someone else can fix their issues. For they know that they are their own source and supply of love. Therefore, they are experiencing health and well-being and abundance flows for their internal state of benevolence is being reflected back at them in their outer world,

Exercise: With your eyes closed and hand on your heart, feel into the vision that you have for you future. Sense and feel that this has already happened and step into the emotion of this vision having already manifested. Feel the love, the joy and all the emotions that you experience as this vision has become a reality and you are fully living it. Truly create a 3D picture of you living your vision and sense the experience of it in sight, sound and all visceral sensations like you are really living this vision.

When we can enter into the field of awareness that this has already happened, then we are a YES inside with our alignment for this to become reality. Remember that you need to match in resonance and vibration to your vision, so this means getting all of your ego self fully out of the way.

If you feel a desire to connect more deeply with the path of Cariad, please connect through our website. This has been a journey and it has been a privilege to share CARIAD CONNECT with you all and it is my deepest wish that you, too will rise in your Sovereign power. If any of you would like to be further involved in our Community Interest Company then you are welcome to become Ambassadors for Cariad if this is calling you, in taking your own 'love in action'. Whatever you choose to do it is about following your own path and letting the heart lead you to your own Divine Truth.

All it takes is the courage to reach out as Lucy has done. For finally able to clear the core beliefs that had her stuck in a life time of addiction, Lucy feels loved now: 'you believed in me', she says, when no one else did. We can all too readily judge and criticise but that is not extending love. When a child has experienced abuse and trauma as Lucy did, they feel that they are to blame. Instead of continuing to punish herself, she now is beginning to hold herself with compassion.

Here is my own dream:

> **I have a dream, the day will come, when every baby will be held as sacred.**
> **The birth of every child revered, as a holy and ecstatic moment of joy and peace.**
> **An opportunity for love to fill our hearts to overflowing, our cups so full;**
> **Each one of us will share the bliss of eternal life.**

Our passion, our purpose, our aliveness is the vitality, the essence of divinity that is pulsing vigour and beauty

Be that which is holy and sacred,
come through and greet my body
so that there is integrity within.
Mastering words that bring love
sound untainted by stories.
Standing beloved, in my heart,
I'm serving humanity from the pulse
of my heart centre, hearing sounds of love.
Foxglove opens and invites you closer,
here within lies natural medicine.
As within our divinity is elixir for life,
our pulse vibrates on wings of love.
In this purity of wisdom, miracles occur
as breath completes and fills us all.
River of magic encapsulates energy
circling through the fields surrounding us.
All we need do is breathe in the divine
soaking it up to fill every cell.

Telomeres stretch up as flowers do
reaching for more sunlight, photosynthesis.
Divine beauty touches petal edges
and they smile to her face.
Greet the dawn on cool air currents.
The peace that surpasses all understanding
silently enters the garden, like a snake;
slowly making its way back up the tree.
Arriving now on outstretched branch,
rest here serpent, your work is done,
for women now have risen, dancing
energy, vibrant, alive and ecstatic.
An everlasting flow for all mankind
for once more, beauty is birthed.

Chapter Nine: CARIAD: living as an expression of love, what does this mean for the Evolution of Consciousness and our Planet?

The greatest gift that lies within us is the ability to accept love, this brings about a visceral change within the chemistry of the human body. Richard Rudd, author of the Gene Keys, talks about the irritant, that grain of sand within the oyster shell that becomes a beautiful pearl. Hidden within all of us is the pearl. The Chinese refer to this as the realisation of unity consciousness. Which is interesting because growing up the only precious gem that drew my attention was the pearl. Could it be that the more pain we feel and transform, the more love we will be sensing?

Generally, our children today are being born with far less density and less of the heavy patterning that we have all worked through. That means that shifts are taking place within us all, we are evolving as a species

As this beautiful quote by Reginald A. Ray says:

> **'Who we are in essence is a living field of awakened boundless love'.**

We each need to drop inside and find the peace of meditation or mindful walking in nature, for every answer we will find within ourselves. Another of my favourite poems is by, David Whyte, entitled, Sweet Darkness. This poem reminds us that we need to each find whatever it is that brings us 'fully alive' and follow this every single day, this is all that matters. Just remembering that the aliveness flows because we are aligning with the natural laws of the universe. We need to notice where we are and what we are doiing when we feel the force or pulsation of full aliveness. I find that this happens in sessions with clients, for every encounter is further learning for us both, for we all share the same core beliefs. Every day I am writing poetry, listening to music and meditating or singing and dancing, what is it that brings you fully alive?

LET US ALL MAKE A STAND FOR LOVE

Every day, I give thanks for the work that I do, which is an expression of love in action, as each person steps forward and notices that they are not at peace. The question that I find myself asking daily, beyond looking at the core beliefs that drive human behaviour, is the question about love? A colleague enquired recently 'so are you finding people are receptive when you talk about LOVE'? It is true, I did used to wonder, will folks really want to listen? But each day as I listen to more and more stories, I can see that the common link to each story is heartbreak. It is love that heals a broken heart.

In the healing of the separation from love, that moment when our innocence separates us somehow from love, maybe we fear it, or we reject love or no longer trust love, whatever the belief is, the fact still remains that it is in the returning to love that we are healed.

When we look at many tribal communities, we notice that they 'wear their babies', when born, babies are carried and held, for around 9-12 months or until the baby walks. What does this do? It connects the baby's heart to its mother's heart, and then the baby is in constant heart connection. My belief is that we all want this heart connection. We are yearning for this human connection. Often, we are searching in all the wrong places, but it is this connection, or lack of it, that motivates human behaviour.

To keep it very simple, love connects us and fear separates us. Every day, both men and women share how they are really scared to love, to connect to this vital life force that pulses every heart. What is the fear? What gets in the way of connecting to love?

I share this now, as I have listened to well over 10,000 heart-breaking stories. But I have children and grandchildren and I want them to grow up in a world where they can open their hearts and connect to love every day! What will this require? It requires us to open our hearts and to break out of the self-imposed fear prisons that we create when we live in fear of expressing our Truth. We resist the possibility of heartbreak. But I would rather live with my heart open and love, than remain closed and let life pass by and watch another generation of children grow up afraid to love. Afraid to go and walk on the street after dark or visit another country, is this the world we want our children to experience?

I wrote a poem, many years ago, about standing up for what we believe in and I believe in love! In the words of the poem: **'let us make a bed of human hearts where every child can rest in love'**. So yes, this may well require many more heart-breaking stories to be shared, but it is about making a stand for love. It is about standing together for what we want to share in our world together. I don't know about you, but I want to share love and joy and live with peace in our world. Let us have the courage to share those stories and to name those core beliefs that are keeping us separated from love, for then we can move into heart connection and build that bed of hearts where children can rest in love. We will notice the behaviours that separate us and the ones that bring us together. I am standing for love; will you join me?

Hannah has done just this, shared her love, with her beautiful contribution for our front cover. It was a Mother's Day card for her own mother. Here is a mother holding close the two hearts of both her daughters. We see all the pieces of the heart and it is in the intricate working of our individual human heart that the answer lies. Hannah shares how art has given voice for all parts of herself to be expressed together. Her painting was capturing her own mother's unfaltering love which she says; 'tethered my heart and shone a light through the darkness of my battles with mental health and addiction',

So how can we all be a living expression of love. Learning how we can each do this, teaching our children how to extend love, where can we connect and hold hearts? All of us together.

Let us make a stand for love together and be able to hold those tough conversations and share how we feel and be open and honest, this gives permission for our planet to breathe. This oneness that connects us all together, it is love, so let's get out of our own way and feel the love that connects every human heart.

What is it that breaks your heart in the world? What would you like to use your passion and energy to make a stand for today?

It is our intention to open our own Cariad Centre here in Pembrokeshire. To provide a home from home for those who would like some space for themselves for short and longer stays. An opportunity to live in an eco-house and enjoy beautiful meals all shared with our community. To walk the beautiful coastline here and rest in a little haven of tranquillity. If you would like to volunteer or indeed support us to get our centre open then we would love to hear from you. Through our website www.mamsuk.org you can contact us.

Thank you taking the Cariad journey and let us know if you would like to join a Cariad group or indeed dive deeper, we are here to offer our support and encouragement.

ACKNOWLEDGEMENTS

Hannah Salisbury for our front cover design
www.hannahsalisburyart,com

Huge gratitude for all of teachers and guides (besides my own Higher Self) and here is a list of those who have provided inspiration for this journey. With heartfelt blessings to you all:

> Kim Rosen, Chloe Goodchild, Jules Heavens, Richard Rudd, Rebecca Hanscombe, Anamarta, Laura Simms, Sharon King, Katie Jones, Carolyn Young, Sue Martin and Peter Melchezidek of EGA. And all of the Cariad Community, especially Helena and Lou for reading drafts and sharing their heart-felt wisdom.

Many thanks to Diederik Wolsak for writing the Foreward and offering supervision. He is the founder and programme director of the Choose Again Attitudinal Healing Centre. An international workshop leader and author.

A BED OF HUMAN HEARTS

With your one wild life, you could
sweep the whole world away,
like a tsunami breaking open
the hearts of nations,
too smug to attend
to the day-to-day frivolities of
life and death for mothers

Breathing in to ignite my passion
Breathing in to stand for what I believe in,

I watched the day you were born,
as your head emerged,
into the arms of your mother
you lay, with lips so perfect and pink
'like a rosebud', so divine
you suckle and slurp and drink
the milk of human kindness.

Sweet is the sound of children's laughter,
and the patchwork quilt is warm
on my Grandmother's bed tonight

Let us make a bed of human hearts
for all children to lie upon,
let them simply 'rest in love'

Surrender the arms and the bloodshed
and drink the milk from
my Grandmother's cup,
and sigh as she dozes by the fire,
 cat purring on her lap
asleep beside the hearth.

Warmth and love is what it takes
to heal a broken heart.
Together I am sure, that one
circle of women can ignite the flame,
to stand for what we believe in, and open our arms
with love
for each and every child.

                                              Sara Hunter